I0492195

Social Media Marketing Books: 3 Manuscripts in 1

Easy and Inexpensive Social Media Marketing Strategies to Make Huge Impact on Your Business

Copyright 2018 by Eric J Scott – All rights reserved.

This document is geared toward providing exact and reliable information in regard to the topic and issue covered. The publication is sold with the idea that the publisher is not required to render accounting, officially permitted, or otherwise, qualified services. If advice is necessary, legal or professional, a practiced individual in the profession should be ordered.

– From a Declaration of Principles which was accepted and approved equally by a Committee of the American Bar Association and a Committee of Publishers and Associations.

In no way is it legal to reproduce, duplicate, or transmit any part of this document in either electronic means or in printed format. Recording of this publication is strictly prohibited and any storage of this document is not allowed unless with written permission from the publisher. All rights reserved.

The information provided herein is stated to be truthful and consistent, in that any liability, in terms of inattention or otherwise, by any usage or abuse of any policies, processes, or directions contained within is the solitary and utter responsibility of the recipient reader. Under no circumstances will any legal responsibility or blame be held against the publisher for any reparation, damages, or monetary loss due to the information herein, either directly or indirectly.

Respective authors own all copyrights not held by the publisher.

The information herein is offered for informational purposes solely, and is universal as so. The presentation of the information is without contract or any type of guarantee assurance.

The trademarks that are used are without any consent, and the publication of the trademark is without permission or backing by the trademark owner. All trademarks and brands within this book are for clarifying purposes only and are owned by the owners themselves, not affiliated with this document.

Table of Contents

Social Media Marketing
A Beginner's Guide to Dominating the Market with Social Media Marketing

Social Media Marketing
Strategies to Capture and Engage Your Audience While Quickly Building Authority

Social Media Marketing
Tips + Tricks to Build Credibility

Table of Contents

Social Media Marketing

A Beginner's Guide to Dominating the
Market with Social Media Marketing

Chapter 1

Introduction to Social Media Marketing

The whole world seems to be caught in a compulsive social media frenzy. Everyone is talking about using social media platforms for engaging their audience, increasing credibility, and building solid brands. There's a marked shift from selling to building relationships, which the social media sites do remarkably well. By definition, social media marketing is nothing but a method of gaining traffic or audience attention for your business through the use of social media. The strategy usually involves concentrating marketing efforts on creating highly engaging content that attracts the attention of your target audience, and encourages them to share it throughout their virtual networks.

Unlike traditional marketing channels, social media marketing doesn't focus on hard selling (though there can be exceptions based on the nature of your business). It is about leveraging the power of audience relationships and forging strong connections through engagement. Social media marketing is about constantly growing your audience base by creating insightful and compelling content. It helps marketers build dramatic brands, fosters customer loyalty, and lays the foundation for selling.

Think of your social media marketing as glamorous toppings on the pizza of your marketing mix. They add more punch and panache to your marketing efforts. Social media marketing makes your marketing techniques more interesting, creative, and appealing to your target audience. It adds a more personal character to your robotic marketing efforts.

Let's take a real life example to establish how social media marketing works. You walk into a department store to buy lipstick or perfume. The salesperson at the counter quickly tries to understand what you want and launches into a tiresome and monotonous script about how XYZ is the bestselling fragrance or lipstick currently. You get frustrated with the whole thing because they are showing you everything that you don't want. The salesperson is not actually helping you buy, but rather trying to sell what they think you should buy. They haven't listened to you or tried to tune in to your requirements. Finally, you move to another store.

At the next store, the salesperson sees you and gives you a warm smile. They chat with you cheerily about your day and the weather. You feel the warmth and friendliness of a real person after talking to them. They take sufficient time to understand exactly what you want by asking you questions related to your lifestyle, preferences and habits. So, do you work very long hours and want a lip color or fragrance that lasts long? Is your style bold, or subtle? Do you enjoy attention, or are you content with toiling diligently in the background?

They talk to you, size you up to understand your needs, and make you feel comfortable. They also offer brilliant tips about how you can make your lipstick last even longer or how certain fragrances can enhance memory and brain functions by stimulating the olfactory glands. In the end, you've had such an enriching experience that you end up buying everything they recommend.

Why? What did the salesperson in the second store do that the one in the first store didn't? They simply connected with you, engaged you in a meaningful conversation, and shared valuable information. Rather than selling you something, they helped you.

Social media marketing is just the same. It is about striking meaningful connections with potential and existing customers to help them buy products and services. Social media marketing is about creating things that excite your customer and makes him think, "Wow, I really want to buy from them." It is about clearing assembly line styles of marketing clutter and replacing it with more personal and relevant messages.

When people like you, they invariably buy from you. Surveys have consistently proved that people buy from brands which they like and can relate to. Before potential customers can turn into loyalists, they need to feel a sense of affinity with your brand. They need to believe your brand values are synonymous with their own. When customers experience a sense of shared belonging with your brand, it won't take much time for them to turn into brand evangelists.

Social media marketing is also significant from the perspective of establishing your authority. It helps you place yourself as an expert in a domain. It reinforces your knowledge and expertise in a specialized niche. Social media marketing lets you position yourself as an influential authority who knows a lot about what you are selling. This automatically increases the credibility and trustworthiness of your brand. People flock to anyone who does justice to the expert tag consistently.

Sharing insightful, thought-provoking, and well-researched matter in your business field makes you come across as someone who is up-to-date with trends within the industry.

Sharp, analytical, and detailed posts present you in a rather flattering light to your target audience. After a while, they start looking forward to your posts on current trends, and they'll engage with you by posing queries and actively soliciting your opinion. All this leads to the creation of an exceptionally credible brand.

Everything else being same (quality and features of product/services etc.), the single most important factor today while making purchasing decisions is customer experience. Customer experience supersedes most other considerations when it comes to buying.

People may compromise on the quality of the product, but they are highly unlikely to overlook an unfavorable customer experience.

Customers like to buy from people who know their material. They prefer buying from sellers who go beyond offering standard products and services and additionally provide slick, new-age value in terms of attractively packaged information and useful tips that make life easier.

Consumers buy from brands they can trust and relate to. Among the hordes of businesses that are trying to garner their attention, customers are most likely to give their money to brands that radiate higher trustworthiness and a personal touch.

Selling is as much about inspiring your buyer's confidence in your brand as it is about extolling the virtues of your products/services. Social media offers you multiple tools, features, and opportunities to do just that – inspire faith in your buyers by building connections through engagement. Let them know you want to help them buy; don't just sell to them.

Social media has traversed far greater heights than simply being a medium for user-generated content. Today, it's a tool for consumer empowerment (we all witness big conglomerates being brought to their knees by that one dissatisfied tweet or widely shared post) and a gratifying brand-consumer partnership.

Even companies that have long been dismissing social media as frivolous and flippant have started taking note of its benefits. They've realized that social media is not limited to games and light-hearted opinion polls (which are also hugely successful in creating affable brands), but can involve more serious discussions and insights that are invaluable when it comes to building strong brands.

One of the best things about social media is that it is amazingly varied and versatile. Some platforms like Pinterest and Instagram are invaluable tools for visually inclined businesses like home décor, cooking, and graphic artists. Meanwhile, channels like LinkedIn and Google+ are ideal for corporate buzz sharing. Twitter and Facebook are flexible enough to be used by businesses of almost all types.

With some ingenuity and resourcefulness, even small businesses can create a storm over social media.

Unlike traditional marketing mediums, social media doesn't swallow a huge chunk of your advertising and promotion budget. You don't need to create cost-intensive and ineffectual marketing plans that leave you broke.

All you need is some creativity, perceptiveness, and an intuitive understanding about your audience's needs. More than sharp business acumen, you need a human touch. Social media gives your brand a human angle without breaking the bank.

Have you seen any of the Whole Foods videos posted on their corporate Facebook page? They frequently post how-to videos in a subject that their customers are primarily interested in – cooking. The short videos, running for about 40-60 seconds, cover multiple elements such as animation, images, and text. At the end of the video, there is an item for sale that customers can buy to prepare the recipe mentioned in the video.

One such inventive video demonstrated how customers could transform leftover Thanksgiving turkey into—hold your breath—nachos. What a refreshing change from the same old boring sandwiches! It isn't surprising that these videos are hugely popular and the products mentioned at the end are quickly grabbed up by eager viewers. They must be doing something right!

Rather than using long-winded sales pitches to glorify their products, Whole Foods is adding value to their followers' lives by sharing insanely creative ideas and making life more convenient for them. The company is showing customers ways through which their products can actually benefit them. Ingenious? Yes. Simple? Doubly yes.

Though it seems overwhelmingly complex for a beginner, especially given all the information available over the Internet, social media marketing can be relatively simple and effective.

You really do not have to be a marketing expert to master social media. All you need is some inventiveness, unwavering enthusiasm to keep learning new trends, and an empathetic touch to understand your audience.

Let's do a quick round-up of the benefits of social media marketing.

1. *Enhances Brand Recognition* – Social media gives you endless opportunities to build your brand by increasing visibility. These platforms act as the "voice" of your brand to forge meaningful communication with customers. It serves a two-fold purpose of making your brand look more accessible to prospective customers and making it more familiar for existing customers.

For instance, a regular Facebook user could know about your company by coming across a post in their newsfeed. Similarly, a more non-involved existing customer may turn into a loyal customer after witnessing your powerful presence on several networks.

Put yourself in your customer's shoes. Imagine picking between two similar brands that offer almost the same quality and features. Which one will you pick? The one that has a powerful social presence across platforms or one who hardly engages with customers on social channels?

2. *Increases Brand Loyalty* – A recent report published by Texas Tech University confirms what we all probably know too well by now—brands that engage with customers on social media enjoy greater loyalty. Companies that take advantage of social media tools to connect with their audience are more likely to inspire loyalty and positive buyer connections.

A strategic and flexible social media plan can easily convert new customers into loyal evangelists. A Convince & Convert study recently concluded that 53% of Americans who follow various brands on social media tend to buy from those brands. Obviously, there is direct correlation between social media engagement (yes, even the seemingly frivolous polls, games, and contests) and customer loyalty.

3. *Provides Greater Brand Authority* – Regular engagement with existing customers is a great way to

inspire the faith of new customers. When people want to boast about your products and services or applaud you for it, they take to social media.

New members within their circle are attracted enough to follow you. The higher the buzz about your products and services on social media, the more authoritative and credible your brand comes across. If you can engage with other high-ranking brands in the field, your visibility and authority can quickly skyrocket.

4. *Reduces Marketing Costs* – Imagine paying for a thirty-second television advertisement prime time slot (nope, your target audience members are not late television watchers) or hiring outdoor advertising space on a prominent city billboard? How much would that set you back? Probably thousands of dollars, with mostly unimpressive results.

Enter social media marketing. For virtually nothing, you can target customers anywhere on the planet. Creating great content, engaging your audience, driving traffic to your website, and boosting sales conversions isn't cost-heavy on social media platforms. You simply need to be people-savvy, create interesting interactions, and understand how to utilize various tools for optimum benefit.

5. *Raises Search Engine Rankings* – Among other complicated factors search engines use to determine the rank or placement of a web page on their search results,

social signals can be one of the most important. When you optimize your posts (with the right keywords, title tags, and meta description) and distribute links pointing to your site throughout social media, you increase your brand signal.

Increased social media activity boosts your authority signal in the eyes of search engines, thus giving you higher rankings on searches when people are actively soliciting products and services related to your niche.

6. *Provides Better Audience Insights* – Few other marketing channels give you the power to target your audience like social media. Businesses can easily target people based on what they follow, their demographics, preferences, and hobbies and interests.

Social media is a great platform from which to gather deeper insights into your customer behavior. Using these insights, you could create products that better suit their compelling needs. Rather than spending astronomical sums targeting all and sundry, hoping and praying that at least some of it yields results, social media allows you to hit the bull's eye.

7. *Improves Customer Service* – Unsurprisingly, a Forbes study revealed that 71% of customers who received a prompt response on social media are more likely to endorse the company's products and services to others.

Social media offer speedy, personal, and direct communication channels for businesses to interact with consumers for problem resolution and other queries.

Unlike other forms of customer service, social media allows other people to view your response in a more open format, thus increasing a brand's transparency and credibility. If you handle an issue faced by a customer remarkably well, you are on your way to earning new customers.

8. *Eases Content Distribution* – Social media dramatically eases the process of content distribution. It can allow you to disseminate your content across a range of platforms to reach a large number of target audiences in the shortest possible span of time.

With the click of a few buttons, content spreads like wildfire across social media. Referral traffic is huge on social media, and content can be quickly disseminated to a high number of targeted folks.

Ensure that your content is aligned with your brand values and the preferences and interests of your target audience. According to consumer psychology, it takes around six to eight exposures for a person to make a decision about purchasing a product.

The use of social media gives that vital repeat exposure to consumers, constantly reminding them about your products and services. Thus, your sales funnel is considerably shortened.

9. *Positions You as an Industry Influencer* – Your influence keeps soaring as you gain new followers. The higher the number of followers on your brand's social media networks, the more credible, valuable, and dependable your brand will come across to potential customers. With a constant inflow of authoritative content, you can position yourself as a leading industry expert who knows what they're talking about.

People are more likely to purchase from experts who have proven their expertise with intelligent and thought-provoking insights over people who simply sell their products. Interaction with other big names in your industry also flatters your brand's profile and lends it more authenticity.

The more value you offer your readers, the more likely they are to return the favor by sharing your content and buying from you.

10. *Increases Conversion Opportunities* – Every post on social media awards you umpteen conversion opportunities. You have the chance of interacting with and targeting new, old, and potential customers with each shared video, image, blog or even a comment.

You never know which reaction may lead to customers visiting your site and ultimately buying something. That's the beauty of social media! Each interaction holds potential for a sale, without directly selling to your customers.

Even when customers do not make immediate purchases, they register the positive interaction for future buying decisions, eventually leading to a conversion.

If you have a large number of followers, the sales can be considerable even with low click-through rates (the percentage of visitors to a website page following a hyperlink text to a specific site, calculated by Total Clicks on the Ad/Total visitors to the page).

The number of potential customers turning into actual customers (conversion rate) is also high on social media due to the humanization factor.

People love brands that display a human element by sharing their behind-the-scenes-stories and engaging with customers. Social media is a platform that allows brands to be people and to have a personality. People like to do business with people, not faceless brands.

Audience building on social media can dramatically boost your existing traffic and, eventually, your conversion rates as well.

Chapter 2

Facebook Marketing for Newbies

Currently, Facebook has an estimated base of 1.71 billion active users. Imagine the amount you are leaving behind on the table if you are not utilizing this powerful social media platform for promoting your brand.

Whether you use it as a free marketing or paid advertising tool, Facebook has the potential to help you reap rich dividends by giving you an incisively targeted customer base of people who are interested in your products and services.

According to a report published by Business2Community, 70% of marketing professionals use Facebook to attract new customers, and 47% of marketers name Facebook as the topmost influencer for purchase decisions. From a bare-bones college community, the social media giant has re-shaped the way we hold online interactions.

Facebook is primarily based on connections. It is all about building connections with old friends, colleagues, family, alumni networks, and of late it even helps build professional connections. Its sheer customization, visibility, and privacy settings give people a lot of choice and control over their interactions. You can choose to make certain posts visible only to specific people and choose who can view what on your profile.

Beyond individual profiles, even brand pages, groups, events pages, communities, and business pages have innumerable customization options for marketers to play around with.

Setting Up a Presence on Facebook

Planning and preparation is key before establishing a solid Facebook presence. Flesh out your brand personality before you set shop on Facebook.

This includes a logo, a clear communication style (for example, decide if you want a more humorous or officious style based on your brand values), recognizable branding with the use of design and color (Coca-Cola's Facebook page is a revelation where branding in concerned), a clear USP (unique selling point), and a thorough knowledge of your target audience.

These elements should also be consistent throughout all marketing and promotional channels, including other social media platforms, blogs, corporate websites, and so on.

Once you're through with the planning stage, set up a Facebook company page (can be groups or communities if you aren't keen on selling immediately but are more inclined toward building a solid community which can be sold to later). Here are some basic requirements once you set up your company page.

1. Get a professional designer to create professional, memorable, and meaningful logos, profile images and cover photos for your page. Make sure that the images are unique and congruent with your overall brand personality.

2. Ensure you have a professional, compelling, and articulate About Us section that best describes your company's background, products and services, and USP.

3. Mention important details such as the business's opening hours, email, contact number, physical address (if available), and other details your customers may want to know.

4. Have a few posts ready before you create your page. These may be curated content (content syndicated from other sites/blogs), images to gather reactions, appealing videos that can be widely shared, and insightful blogs posts.

5. Use high resolution images for describing your products and services along with pithy and interesting descriptions to go along with them. Keep your product and service descriptions brief, attention-grabbing, and informative.

6. Preferably, have a specific person or group of people manage your Facebook account to maintain a consistent voice and persona.

Gain a Skyrocketing Following and Audience Engagement

Now that the basics are in place, here's where the real leg work begins. Gaining followers can be both easy and tricky depending on your understanding of your target audience. Here are some killer tips for helping to gain an avalanche of followers.

1. To begin with, invite existing people within your Facebook network, including family, friends, employees, business associates, etc. to like and follow your page. Once you have a decent following, it will be easier to enlist the support of outsiders.

People are naturally attracted to pages that have an established following, and tend to give pages with low or no following a miss. Hence, ensure that everybody from your network is invited and covered. An option to invite your friends to like a page is present on the page itself. Simply click on it and check friends whom you want to invite to the page by clicking their names.

2. Next, you can start following other big names in your industry, along with people and groups who you think may be interested in your products and services. Ensure that you don't mix up your personal profile and business page. In the admin panel, located on top of your page, click on edit and select "Use Facebook as (your business name)."

Like all relevant groups, communities, and pages across your category. Leave messages, actively comment on their posts and share content to draw attention. Before you do all this, ensure that you read the rules of pages and groups to avoid being banned from them forever.

You may find the odd company that's hostile while interacting with competitors, but this is more of an exception than the rule. Most businesses on social media recognize the value of industry networking by building online connections.

3. One grave mistake most beginning Facebook marketers make is focusing solely on gaining likes over increasing engagement. Engaging followers with your posts is as crucial as expanding your follower base. Social signals based on increased page activity are more important than mere likes.

A higher follower base can obviously help you boost engagement, but simply concentrating on acquiring new followers while failing to engage existing ones is a surefire way to Facebook marketing disaster.

4. User engagement is hugely influenced by the timing and frequency of your posts. If your posts aren't garnering enough reactions and/or shares, ask yourself if you are posting when your target audience is actually available to respond to those posts. Focus on engaging your customers at particular times.

For Facebook, the best time to post is during noon. Morning and evening rush hour timings are also great from the engagement perspective. Studies have revealed an 18% greater engagement rate on Thursday and Friday.

Though there have been differing opinions, most experts agree that 1pm to 3pm is a good time for scheduling Facebook posts for higher engagement and click-through rates. Lunch breaks, rush hours, and post-dinner hours are tested to be a good time for audience involvement. You may have to consider time zones if you are targeting customers across different states and countries.

A Buddy Media study has revealed that pages which post about one to two posts a day enjoy 40% more user engagement than pages that post more than thrice a day. This clearly establishes that the social media audience seeks more quality than quantity.

5. One of the best tips for increasing your followers is an absolute no-brainer, yet you'd be surprised how many people actually overlook it. Check your successful and widely followed competitor pages to see what they are doing to draw audience. Some of the insights you gain using this method can be extremely revealing.

Since the nature of every business is different, there cannot be a standard set of ideas for engaging followers on Facebook. A strategy that can work miraculously for one business may be an absolute disaster for another. Find pages similar to yours doing a basic Facebook or Google searches and emulate their audience engagement strategies for gaining new followers.

6. Create original, valuable and attention-grabbing content. Post content that is useful or simply fun for your target audience. Make your blog posts detailed, grammatically correct, well-researched, and hugely impressive before sharing them on social media. People love to share information or posts that make them come across as smart among online social networks (referred to as social currency in Johan Berger's book Contagious, which discusses why things catch on).

If you create content that increases the "social currency" of your target audience within their circle of influence, they are more likely to share it. People love to flaunt the fact that they are up-to-date with information about things that affect them and their peers. Cash in on this syndrome by creating unique, focused, and compulsively readable content. Back your posts with professional and high resolution images that match the overall sentiment of the post.

To keep your credibility from shattering, check all content for grammatical errors and factual discrepancies. Do not share content originating from dubious sites. In short, don't do anything that will take away from your awesomeness. Pro tip: Infographics are one of the most widely shared content formats. Create comprehensive, industry-relevant and detailed infographics using infogr.am.

7. Check what's catching on like wildfire. Buzzsumo is a great place to check out what's going viral in your niche. Once you are aware of the topics received well by people, create posts centered on the same theme or idea.

For instance, if you run a travel business related page, you may come to realize that some of the most widely shared posts on Facebook according to Buzzsumo are those related to pet travel. There, now you have a bagful of content ideas that can be shared by a passionate pet traveling community. If you want higher engagement and shares, avoid hackneyed content and scour for new angles. People quickly lap up novelty.

8. Place a Facebook Page Plugin prominently on your blog or website to make it easy for readers to follow you on Facebook. Like buttons next to blog posts are great for

sharing content but the page plugin will help increase the actual page likes and increase your following.

Promoting your Facebook page across different social networks such as LinkedIn or Twitter is also an astute move. People won't be pushed into taking action with a mere "Like Us On Facebook" button. You may have to divert your connections (followers) to conversations happening on your Facebook page.

9. Engage with similar pages within your industry. You can frequently leave behind thought-provoking, smart, and well-researched comments on other pages.

Responding intelligently or humorously to posts on other highly followed pages will make their followers sit up and take notice of your page. This not only helps you develop a rapport with other pages and build industry connection networks, but also boosts your page engagement. Ensure that you comment using your business page and not your personal profile.

Another little known insider tip is to tag similar pages in your posts. This way your post appears on the walls of other pages, thus sparking an interest among their founders and fans.

10. Always enable the similar page suggestions option in your settings. This is another lesser known yet highly effective trick for attracting lots of free likes for your page.

When a user likes your competitor's page, Facebook automatically recommends your page to them under "similar page suggestions." All you need to do is enable your "similar page suggestions" option, which can be located in the page's settings.

11. Contests, freebies, and giveaways are great ways to get your audience to share posts on Facebook. Post monthly or weekly giveaways to entice people to share your post with their friends.

Contest and freebie posts spread rapidly, and can quickly help you skyrocket your following. You can ask people to like your page, comment on the thread, share the post on their wall, or tag their friends to qualify for the giveaway.

Don't make it too complicated and time-consuming. Liking the page and sharing should be the basic requirement. Get creative and come up with something that holds the interest of your target audience.

For example, if you deal in baby products, you could have a cutest baby contest by asking parents to like your page, post images of their baby in the comments section, and share your post. This way you are reaching hundreds of friends of every single parent who participates.

This is more cost effective than monumental advertising budgets, and insanely interesting! Keep coming up with creative contests and giveaways to increase audience participation and sharing.

Another great way to garner more likes is to offer your Facebook fans and followers exclusive insider discounts for liking your page. According to a Syncapse study, 42% of respondents admitted to liking pages for discounts and money-saver coupons.

12. Follow the 80-20 content rule when it comes to posting on Facebook. This means reserving 80% of your posts for informational and engaging content, while devoting only 20% to promotional content. This ratio will vary, depending on your business. On the whole, however, this is a good strategy to follow.

As discussed earlier, social media is not a platform for selling per se. It is more a channel for creating a build-up to the sale by forging strong connections with your audience.

13. Referencing your Facebook page in your blog posts is a great way to direct readers to your page. People don't simply like clicking on buttons that say "like us" or "follow us." They follow pages when there's something interesting in it for them.

If you've had a particularly interesting discussion on a Facebook post, go ahead and reference it by linking to the post from your blog. People who are reading your blog are already interested in your products or services, and will be more eager to check out discussions related to the blog post.

14. Create topical groups. Sometimes, consumers are wary of liking brand pages. It's not like they don't buy stuff, they are just tired of receiving marketing messages and seek more meaningful engagements. Get these folks involved with topical Facebook groups.

Create a group related to your industry that may interest your target audience. Say a group for mothers if you are into child care products or a group for car enthusiasts if you are a distributor of automobile parts.

Groups may not help your branding strategy as much as a proper business page, but you will most likely enjoy higher engagement. People like to participate in predominantly non-promotional groups that add more value to their life.

If you are looking to build relationships, trust, and connections over simply peddling your goods and services, groups may be a better bet. They may not have a uniform voice or tone, but they can be far more interesting and flexible than a regular business page.

15. Keep your Facebook posts short and appealing. Research conducted by Blitzlocal has suggested that shorter Facebook posts (100-120 characters) are likely to attract the highest audience engagement.

Users on the Internet have a limited attention span, with hundreds of businesses trying to capture interest. People do not spend more than few seconds to size up your post and decide if it's worth their while to get involved in your content.

Posts that are short, snappy, and out of the ordinary are likely to enjoy greater engagement than elaborate and verbose material. Asking short, direct, and thought-provoking questions is a great way to spark dialogues and get people to respond on Facebook.

16. Equip yourself with the image arsenal. A picture is worth more than a thousand words on Facebook. Images are a superb way to attract customers and build engagement. They help your posts stand out from uninspiring links and wordy status updates.
Clear, bright, and eye-catching images instantly increase the desirability of your products and services. They are also more digestible than long-winded textual posts for attention-starved users.

A ladies' fashion apparel brand, Leneys, uses the power of images brilliantly to engage their audience. They frequently post multiple images and ask followers to pick their favorite attire. A single such post garnered them more than 50 comments, 55 shares, and an impressive 52 likes.

Ensure that you don't steal photos by taking them from a Google image search. There are a lot of copyright laws related to images on the Internet and you could get into serious legal trouble if you use photographs and images without permission of the creators.

Instead, use images you create, buy images from stock photo sites, or use free images from sites such as Pixabay (read their terms and conditions carefully). You can also use images from Wiki Commons with proper attribution (read rules carefully as they vary from image to image).

17. Use "Call-to-Action" effectively for greater engagement. Calls to action are essentially psychological nudges which propel customers to respond. These may not necessarily be related to taking a purchase-related action, but simply ask your customers to respond in some way to what you've posted.

Taking the discussion above from how attention-depraved social media users are, let's make it easier for them to react by giving them specific details about how to respond.

What exactly do you want your followers to do? Comment on a post? Share or like it? Create posts that help them do exactly what you want them to do.

Take an example of Subway's Facebook page. They keep posting beautiful images and include a simple yet powerful "Call-to-Action" to get customers to react. One such post had an image of a beautiful beach along with a caption asking users to "like" the post if they wished to spend their

Sunday on a beach. Now, it doesn't take a genius to figure out that most people would enjoy lazy weekend beach trips.

However, how many people actually think of getting their users engaged by asking them something so obvious? Very few. The post gathered more than 53,000 likes and over 400 shares. Not bad, right?

You have to guide people into doing what you want them to do without making it too apparent. Post things that your target audience is passionate about, or something that drives them.

18. Inject wit and humor into your posts. Everyone loves a good laugh in the midst of day-to-day stress (little wonder that those cat and dog dancing videos are so popular). Humor lends a more personal and informal tone to your interactions.
Though it may vary from business to business, virtually any type of business can inject humor into their posts to make them more fun and appealing.

People love the positive vibes of a feel good and humorous post, and these happy vibes are ultimately transmitted to your brand. They instantly associate your brand with positivity and cheer, thus rendering it more likeable.

Take the example of how Groupon converted a potentially embarrassing post into a downright hilarious affair, which was widely shared across various social media platforms as an epitome of social media expression. They posted an image of rather risqué looking banana holders. Users were obviously thrilled at the prospect of trolling them, little knowing what was in store for them.

Rather than replying caustically to the trolls, their bunch of social media superstars came up with insanely funny comebacks for each comment. For instance, Jane's comment, "What if our bananas are too big?" was met with, "Don't exaggerate." It made for a fun read and you bet all their banana holders were completely sold out.

18. Crowdsource for queries. Another whopper of a tip for increasing your engagement is to allow other users to answer questions rather than answering it yourself. Natural Parenting Tips has mastered this strategy rather well. As the name suggests, it is a page that focuses on offering parenting advice and tips.

Each day they post their fans' questions, while inviting others to help. The idea is to gather suggestions, advice, and tips from their parent fan base. This not just helps the fan who has asked the question, but also other parents. Give this tip a try and witness how active your fans can be when it comes to offering advice about something they can closely relate to.

Chapter 3

The Beginner's Guide to Pinterest

Social media's image-conscious player, Pinterest, has got everyone raving, and with good reason. The site is nothing but a virtual counterpart of pin boards that we've all used for collecting our favorite images and write-ups.

Pinterest has lent a pretty glamorous sheen to a simple, everyday concept. It invites users to create "pinboards" for selecting and sharing images, videos, and write-ups related to their interests. With close to 100 million unique users, the site is slated to grow phenomenally in coming years. It is currently the third largest social media site, just after Facebook and Twitter.

In average minutes spent per month on the site, Pinterest is second only to Facebook. Pinterest users spend an average of 89 minutes per month creating and browsing pinboards, while Facebook records an average of 405 minutes per user each month. Impressive? You bet.

However, some businesses still fail to capitalize on the unique and interesting features of Pinterest simply because they don't realize how it can add value to their business. Here's everything you need to know to get started.

Let's understand some basic Pinterest lingo first

Pin – This is the visual counterpart of a Facebook or Twitter post. These posts are in the form of images that are added from various blogs and websites by clicking on the 'Pin It' button. You can also upload your own images from a computer or other devices. Every pin added by clicking on the "Pin It" option can take users back (links to) to the site/blog it originated from.

Board – This is a compilation of pins focused on a single theme or topic. For instance - kitchen décor, cocktails, DIY crafts for kids, and other similar topics. Think of it as the virtual version of image boards.

Following – "Following All" allows of the pins and boards of a particular user to show up on your timeline. If you are interested in what someone pins, all you have to do is follow their account. Followers, on the other hand, are those who follow your pins or a specific board.

Repin – A Repin is simply adding pins that you find by browsing through Pinterest to your board. The user who originally pinned the image gets attributed each time their image is repinned. Repins keep the link to the original blog or website intact, irrespective of the repinned numbers.

The Pinterest Home Page

The home page is the first thing you'll come across after you register and sign in. This page has a main board, which is a selection of all followed pins. It is similar to a Twitter or Facebook feed or stream. The main board is called the Following Board. It features all the pins from the various boards you follow, including the number of likes, comments, and repins the original pin has garnered.

On the homepage's upper left corner, there are updates about Recent Activity that shows if anyone started following the boards and pins you created, liked your pin, or repinned a pin.

Other than the pins you are already following, the homepage allows you to filter other pins. You can pick categories that you want to see. For instance, if you select "Travel," you'll be able to see the pins and boards which are tagged with a matching description.

The "All" section is a single board that pulls in every user's images and pins. "Popular Pins," on the other hand, features pins that have garnered the highest number of likes, comments, or repins. These can be seen as the trending Pinterest pins.

The home page also features a unique "Gifts" section. It's pretty similar to the "Everything" option, with the exception that all pins added here come with a price tag.

Any pin with an attached price is by default added to the "Gifts" section (for example, a $10-30 price range). All you have to do to include a pin in "Gifts" is add a price in the description. If you are looking for a specific Pinterest account, use the search bar located in the top-left corner.

How to Create a Pinterest Board

Step 1: For creating a Board, go to Add on the top right corner of the site and click on Create Board.

Step 2: Give the board a title and pick a relevant category. Picking the right category is crucial as it will help users locate your boards easily while scouring for Interests.

How to Add and Upload a Pin

Step 1: Click Add and select the Add a Pin option.

Step 2: Paste the URL to be posted and click on Find Images.

Step 3: Pinterest will launch a search for all images within the article. Ensure the post has a relevant title. Click Pin It and share the pin on the appropriate board within the drop down menu options.

For uploading pins, you simply click on Upload a Pin by going to Add in the top right corner of your page.

Killer Pinterest Marketing Tips for Beginners

Get Creative – The entire medium of Pinterest in based on creativity and visual appeal. The several businesses that view Pinterest as a predominantly crafts and cooking platform can take a cue from GE. The nature of their services isn't something you'd immediately associate with Pinterest.

However, they frequently update their feed with superbly inspiring boards dedicated to kitchen ideas, geeky gifts, and more. With some ingenuity, virtually any business can harness the power of this visually captivating social network.

Include Relevant Details – Sometimes people are all set to buy the pinned items they come across. Simply add a price to your pinned or repinned images to make it easier for users. Pins with prices attached are said to gather 36% more likes than those without price tags.
However, ensure that you aren't just selling. Make your boards a nice combination of utility, ideas, and sales. Most

users are browsing for ideas and inspiration, which should be given to them if you want to attract more followers.

Humanize Your Brand Visually – You may want to check Ben and Jerry's as an exemplary example of how they've captured the behind-the-scenes human aspect of their brand by sharing details about the brand's history, the stories of their employees, and more.

The jam-packed marketing world could do with breath of fresh air in the form of fuzzy, feel-good human stories. This adds a more personal touch to your marketing campaign and ensures greater brand loyalty.

Repin the Most Successful Pins – One of the best strategies that businesses often fail to capitalize on is repining pins that are hot and gathering plenty of attention on Pinterest. Repinning the most popular pins will increase repins.

These may not promote your blog post or website, but your followers will get into the habit of visiting your profile and repinning pins selected by you. Once they view your profile, it won't take them much time to start repinning your original pins, which can give you considerable exposure.

Pin Blog Posts ¬– Relationships on social media are built by value. Offers your visitors value, and they are likely to stick with you. Help them get that value from you by simplifying the actions you want them to perform. Trust is built only when people consistently discover the value you offer.

Pin your blog posts by scheduling them for the most optimal times. For Pinterest, the best time to pin something is 2pm, 4pm and 8pm. Include a short summary for the blog post along with appropriate keywords (to make it easily traceable in search engine results).

Go Beyond the Niche – Pinterest is a brilliant platform to showcase your hobbies and interests, along with a professional profile. Go beyond your professional avatar to pin a more personal picture for your followers. Everyone likes to see the "real person" behind a professional persona. Include your hobbies, personality traits, and interests in the bio. Engage in conversation with people who share similar interests.

You will have a field day discussing felines with fellow cat fans if you mention "cat lover" in your Pinterest bio. Shared interests create a greater sense of belonging, thereby increasing the chances of users eventually buying from you.

Participate in Group Boards – Imagine if you could promote something to thousands of people without too much effort. Group boards are a boon for people who want to gain a following by contributing. The reason why group boards are so insanely popular on Pinterest is because when a user participates in group board, the board automatically appears on their profile.

When new followers click the "Follow All" option, the user follows each board within a profile, including group boards. People want a higher number of users within a group, since higher contributions means more engagement and greater exposure. Therefore, getting accepted into groups can be quite easy. Once in a group, your profile is easily accessible to the thousands of followers within that group. Works both ways, right?

You profile ends up looking more attractive with a nice assortment of updated boards. When you pin on a high activity group board, you are tapping into a large audience base and getting more followers in the bargain.

Create Optimized Descriptions – Pinterest gives you a maximum of 500 characters, though you shouldn't make your posts that long. Users on Pinterest prefer pithy and snappy posts, where images do all the talking. Keep the description a little over a Tweet (200-250 characters should be your hot spot) for eliciting maximum repins.

Ensure that your description is optimized with appropriate keywords, a couple of hashtags, and most importantly, a Call-to-Action such as clicking on the image to visit the blog or article.

Hashtags and keywords are essential if you want users to easily locate your pins using the platform's search engine.

This leads to better exposure for your brand. And who doesn't need more spotlight?

Bring the Influencer's Leverage – Use the power of influencers to build awareness about your brand by collaborating with them on busy group boards.

This won't just make you profile more flattering, it will also make you come across as someone who is constantly engaging with followers and contributing to the board. A double whammy!

Images Without Faces – Strange as this may seem, images without faces are likely to gather 23% more repins than those with faces. It seems that visually driven users on Pinterest do not want to see pretty faces, but inspiring ideas. Focus on pinning non-people focused images.

Creative ideas, resourcefulness, novelty and inspiration are the key. People use Pinterest as a tool for generating and collecting ideas. Make your pins more idea-centric.

Avoid Spamming Boards with Self-Promotion – Though this may seem like a lovely platform for promoting small and mid-sized enterprises, avoid spamming boards with excessive self-promotion. Pinterest users frown upon too much self-endorsement and are more accepting of people who add value by contributing to the community. It is considered good Pinterest etiquette to link and connect by sharing images that truly inspire your brand's work rather than blatantly selling your products and services.

What things and ideas shape your company's vision? Where do you draw your inspiration from? What is the story behind your brand? Sharing all this will help you build more meaningful connections on Pinterest. Self-promotion, if anything, should be more creative and subtle.

Use the Pinterest platform for building trust, forging a strong community of like-minded folks, and grabbing attention. The platform is more of a community than a place for doing business. People here appreciate each other's recommendations and suggestions. Research has revealed that Pinterest users spend more per referral on Pinterest than any social network.

While shoppers from Facebook average at spending $60-80, Pinterest sits comfortably at $140-180). This means people make more high-end purchases based on recommendations on Pinterest. This should give you enough motivation to create Pinterest promotion campaigns that work!

Tutorials are the Way to Go – Since sharing ideas and helping people is the bedrock of Pinterest, try to help your customers rather than pushing products or services on them. The click-through rate for guides and tutorial-based pins is a staggering 42% more than regular pins; people click on useful things that make their lives easier.

Rather than creating pins about your products or services, why not show users how to use these products or services optimally? If you run an online organic grocery store, rather than promoting the fresh greens, why not share pins of delicious and healthy organic breakfast recipes or inventive organic smoothies? Get the drift? It is all about giving before you take.

Use Warm and Bright Colors – Other than the obvious guideline of using clear and high-quality images, keep in mind that bright and warm toned pictures get twice as many repins than cool colors like blue and green. Try and stick to images bearing flaming colors such as orange, deep red, brown, burgundy, etc. to garner more repins.

Little Known Tools – Like most social media platforms, Pinterest has its own set of valuable tools that can be used to optimize your networking and/or promotional campaigns. Use Viraltag for scheduling pins, while Curalate can help you with audience insights (web traffic stats, engagement levels, and people's response to pins). Pinalerts are great for getting instant notifications about engagement.

Chapter 4

Twitter Marketing for Beginners

Your business needs Twitter. Period. It can be overwhelming for new users with its character limit, frenzied feed, and multiple features. However, being one of the most active and popular social media platforms, there's no way you can ignore it.

A solid Twitter presence gives you access to a huge database of potential customers who can be engaged with a single Tweet. The microblogging giant currently has 313 million active monthly users, and more than 400 million tweets are sent per day. You're leaving a lot of money on the table if you're not harnessing the potential of this versatile and dynamic social media network.

Establish a Clear Strategy

Have a clear social media plan in place before starting on Twitter. What are you aiming to achieve through a Twitter presence? Higher engagement? Building a corporate brand? Better customer service? Networking with other industry professionals? Or all of it? Your overall strategy should be congruent with your marketing or business goals.

Create an Impactful Profile and Cover Image

Your Twitter profile should ideally be your corporate logo or a professional image of yourself. It should be uniform with other social networks, where you already have or are trying to establish a social presence. Get a graphic designer to create a killer logo that packs plenty of punch.

The cover image again should be high-resolution, attention-grabbing, and catchy. It should complement your profile picture and go with the overall brand persona or the "voice" of your brand. Ensure you add your business website (experts recommend using a dedicated Twitter landing page and including it in the profile URL section for a more personal and relevant user experience) and a compelling Call-to-Action. You can keep changing the Call-to-Action depending on the latest trends, products and services, or seasons.

Get Noticed

Your aim on Twitter from day one should be to get noticed for your awesomeness. One of the best ways to do this is by using the hashtag (more on that later). Ensure your hashtags are relevant, snappy, memorable, and interesting. Restrict the number of hashtags to about 2-3 per post, else you risk losing engagement.

Another nice tip to up your desirability quotient is re-tweeting great stuff related to your industry. Include your own attention-grabbing comment about why you think it's worth sharing. Participating and hosting Twitter chat parties is a great way to contribute and engage with a highly focused audience.

Build a Strong Following

One of the best ways to build a following on Twitter is by citing other Twitter influencers in your industry. This will show up on their feed, they will be notified and most likely openly express their gratitude, thus giving you an opportunity to be followed by thousands of their targeted followers.

Stay in tune with the latest trends to create events, hashtags, and topical tweets about them. These can cater to a general as well as niche audience. When you quote tweets of other users or influencers in your blog, inform them. They may share the post with their followers, since well everyone loves to be recognized as an expert. And yippee, you get increased exposure!

Remove Spammy Accounts

Keep evaluating your Twitter following periodically for blocking spammy and dubious accounts. This frequent spring cleaning will ensure you have real, solid, and engaged users rather than a bunch of spammers who can harm your Twitter authority.

Everyone wants to enjoy a high following, but allowing spammy accounts to follow you just to flaunt big numbers is a definite highway to Twitter hell. Having a small group of loyal and genuine followers is better than being followed by thousands of fake and inactive users who can hurt your account.

Voice and Branding

The nature of Twitter is such that you have only 140 characters to make or break your reputation, which means each word matters. Your company's unique voice will trickle into each interaction. So, what should be the ideal tone of your brand? How should you react to customer complaints and conflict?

Should you maintain a more humorous or serious stance through your interactions? You need to decide this beforehand in order to keep interactions in line with your overall brand values and corporate goals. Interactions shouldn't be based on whether you've got your cup of evening coffee, or your mood.

There should be absolute consistency and uniformity in your tone. Over time, this consistency will help followers know what to expect from your interactions with them, which will invariably shape your brand identity or image. It will come to define your fundamental brand persona.

Be Interesting and Addictive

Twitter isn't the medium to be loquacious, though you need to constantly reinforce your presence through interesting and compulsively readable tweets. Let them offer value over being overtly promotional. Offering 50% discount on a newly launched product may seem like an attractive proposition, but followers will soon get tired of seeing your company with the same sales lens. Bring about a shift from marketing to revealing your personal brand by adding value.

Fast food giant Taco Bell has an innately snarky Twitter persona, which is consistently evident in their engaging, humorous, and irreverent tweets. Taco Bell has mastered the art of being bang on their brand identity, and it works wonderfully for them. Look at their content strategy and customer engagement – simply brilliant!

Quick Response Is the Key

What is it they say about the early bird getting the worm? Well, it can't be any truer than on Twitter. It is essential to respond to customer queries and complaints as quickly as possible. Customer service needs rapid attention owing to the speedy pace and condensed nature of the network.

If you take long to reply to a critical tweet, other followers may amplify the single voice, and it may spiral beyond control. That being said, don't just Twitter for damage control or to answer queries. Keep popping up to greet your followers and share positive things. Also, acknowledge the appreciation that comes your brand's way.

Scheduling Twitter Updates

You or your social media manager may not always be available at the time you actually want your tweet to be released. Scheduling updates is a great way to publish tweets when your follower community is active. Obviously, posts related to breaking news such as global disasters or local tragedies will need quick, on-the-spot updates; however, for other more strategically planned updates, you can organize yourself and make your work much easier by scheduling updates.

Replying on Twitter

People generally use the @username to reply to someone on Twitter. A sample of this would look something like:

@username Thank you. I am glad you loved our food!

This will make your Tweet visible only to your followers and the followers of the person/business you've tagged. If you want more people to be able to view the post, use a period or another marker before the @ sign on the username.

Retweeting

Retweeting is simply sharing someone else's tweet with your followers. You simply re-share with your followers what someone else has shared with their followers.

To manually retweet something, you open a separate tweet box and paste the tweet into it. Add RT and the author or company's handle (@username) to display that you've shared someone else's tweet. You can also automatically retweet by clicking on the two arrow options placed between "reply" and "like" below every tweet.

Adding a comment of your own at the top of the retweet is a great way to add your own voice to it.

Educate, entertain, and illuminate your audience with your retweets. In short, add the wow factor or make them smile. You can find interesting and retweetable trivia even for the most officious brands.

For instance, lawyers or law firms can take a break from heavy topics and bring some laughs by retweeting trivia related to the most hilariously outdated laws. Add clever industry related one-liners or tweet something humorous about a current event or trend. Always retain the original source of the tweet if you're retweeting.

Retweeting is good Twitter etiquette because you aren't simply stealing someone else's content, but giving them due credit for it. However, retweet sparingly by choosing only those tweets that stand out or should not be missed by your target audience. Avoid being offensive or controversial.

Create memorable and unique tweets of your own that others would love to retweet. This boosts your brand authority and social signals.

Hashtags

Hashtags present your message to a larger audience. People who may not be following you can follow updates posted by you based on hashtags. Hashtags are like condensed signposts that interestingly capture the essence of your message in a few characters.

The social media phenomenon of hashtagging became so successful and prevalent that it found itself in the Oxford dictionary.

Rather than creating hashtags that promote your business, build hashtags around value propositions and human elements.

Hashtags can range from profoundly meaningful to downright irreverent, as long as it grabs the attention of your target audience. You wouldn't expect something as banal as toilet paper to catch like wildfire on social media, yet Charmin's insanely clever #TweetFromTheSeat did just that. Research indicated that a lot of people access social media from the comfortable confines of their toilet seat. Charmin's creative brains sprang into action and decided to create a campaign where followers were asked to post selfies while being seated on the 'big throne.' Charmin's hashtag campaign became a huge success.

If you follow a few rules when it comes to hashtags, you aren't very far from Twitter glory.

One of the worst things to do is create hashtags that bear the name of your brand. Nope, hashtags aren't meant to do that. That's blatant ego massaging. Keep hashtags compatible with the tone, values and vision of your brand. Dove's #speakbeautiful campaign captured the spirit of the brand's focus on natural, innocent, and real beauty rather well.

Your hashtags should reveal what your brand fervently represents rather than the brand itself. Humanize it. Add fun. Make it personal. People love to participate in discussions on hashtags they can relate to. Your hashtags should be actionable and instantly catchy. Hashtagging is all about reinforcing your brand's personality and not about getting people to worship your brand (though with great hashtags, eventually they will).

Do not make your hashtags complex or difficult to remember. Use desirable, fun, in-vogue words that people can easily remember and relate to. Make it rhyme. Use clever wordplay or puns. Hashtags should make it easy for users to search for your posts. Humanize these tags by associating them with a powerful emotion. Make A Wish's #sffbatkid is a brilliant example of how the foundation promoted a documentary of one of their members to evoke powerful emotions among followers.

When someone retweets your post, acknowledge it by thanking them for it. This way, you are not just establishing yourself as the original author of the tweet but also coming across as more approachable to their followers.

Twitter Parties

Twitter parties allow you to thank your followers and build a loyal community by hosting engaging virtual get-togethers. You may have to determine how to weave this strategy into the nature of your business, since it may not be relevant for all enterprises.

Twitter events are a great way to gather more followers, engage existing followers, and generally create buzz about your products and services without actually selling them. Typically, these Twitter events last between 12 and 24 hours. Hosting them monthly is a great idea to keep the interest factor alive.

Create a catchy and memorable hashtag specifically for the event. You can add videos of previous Twitter parties to let new followers know what's in store for them or spread the word about your new products and services without selling. Trust that people who have fun will act as the ultimate evangelists for your brand.

Step-by-Step Guide on How to Host a Twitter Party or Event

Before you start hosting a Twitter party, zero in on a theme related to your brand. Know exactly what drives your target audience and what they'd really be interested in. Invoking their passions and interests is a great way to get them involved. What's you core objective of hosting the event? Do you want to gain new followers or simply awaken the slumbering folks? Are you testing the market for a potential product, or do you want to create a strong buzz about a newly launched product or service? Working out a clear objective will help you formulate a strategy that's in line with your basic goals.

1. *Pick a Topic* – You need a central theme, topic, or idea that's closely related to your brand for your Twitter party. It should be something powerful that immediately stirs engagement. Contests and training sessions are a great way to give back to your audience.

For instance, if you are into beauty or make-up products or grooming services, you can gather a group of raving make-up lovers for a #funfridaymakeupbash where you and all followers share their favorite make-up secrets over interesting conversation and discussions.

2. *Create a Hashtag* – Use all the points and expert tips mentioned above under the hashtags section to create a unique, memorable, and attention-grabbing hashtag for the event. Keep it simple and relevant.

3. *Schedule the Event* - You will want to schedule your event at a time when your followers are most active on Twitter. This can vary from topic to topic. However, generally speaking 1pm to 4pm Eastern Time is a good time to ensure maximum participation.

4. *Promote the Event* – You have to spread the message about your upcoming event a few days before the event. Inform your followers beforehand to mark the date and keep themselves free during the event hours. This will also allow them to distribute the message among their followers, thus ensuring a sizeable participation for the event.

5. *Plan Your Tweets in Advance* – Of course, wit, spontaneity, and relevant responses are the hallmark of a successful social media event, but you also need to have a ready bank of pre-planned tweets to stir the discussion and conversation in the direction you want. Otherwise, the event might end up being a free-for-all, where everyone other than you is promoting themselves and their products and services.

You need to tactfully control and divert the chat in the direction you want, while also allowing it to flow naturally. Use Buffer or Hootsuite to schedule your Tweets in advance.

6. *Send Out Constant Reminders* – You need to keep reminding your followers about the upcoming event without annoying them. Reminder posts are a good way to put the event on top of their head if they've forgotten about it but are enthusiastic about being a part of it.

7. *Assign Tasks* – You may need more than one person to carry out specific tasks related to the event. For instance, one moderator can monitor tweets, while the other can pick contest winners or respond to participants.

8. *Host the Party* – You need to be extremely attentive, keen, and focused throughout the party. However, that shouldn't stop you from enjoying it. Launch Hootsuite or Buffer to be kept in the loop about the latest social media buzz related to your party.

9. *Send Prizes* – Do not forget to quickly send out the prizes once the event concludes. Ask winners to notify you about their email address through direct messaging. You can add their email address to your mail list for future updates and newsletters.

10. *Obtain Feedback* – What's the point in having a party when you don't get to know what everyone thought about it? Even for regular parties, don't we want to know if our guests had a great time? Create a survey or send out an email to obtain feedback about the event. Analyze what you did well and what you can do better, and incorporate the necessary suggestions in your next virtual bash.

Chapter 5

Instagramming for Social Media Success

Instagram features more than 400 million users with over 70 million images shared every day. More than 90% of Instagram users are under 35 years of age. This should be enough reason for you to make it a component of your social media mix. Here's a complete beginner's guide for Instagram marketing success.

Download the Instagram App – Download the Instagram app from the app store. You will have to sync the app with your iOS device if you are downloading from iTunes.

Create an Account – Click on "Sign Up" at the bottom of the app screen to enter all details such as your username, password, email, and, optionally, your phone number. You can add a brief and interesting personal or company introduction under the "About" section. Ensure that you include your business or personal website.

Follow Friends – You can either import contacts and located friends from your existing contact list or manually search for friends using their usernames. Following people allows you to view their updates on your feed. Just like with Twitter, you can follow people who you don't personally know such as celebrities and international figures.

Click "Next" once you are done. Instagram will suggest some users based on the users you are already following. You can follow these suggestions by clicking "Follow" adjacent to their usernames.

The New Instagram Direct Update – The recent Instagram update allows users to choose who they want to share their pictures with. Sometimes, you may not want to share every image with all your followers. This lets you customize settings about who gets to see what about your public feed.

Scrolling and Discovering Photos – Tap on the house-like icon on the left bottom toolbar. You can now scroll through all new posts of users you follow. There's a Discovery tab represented by a magnifying glass on top of the page. You can search for hashtagged posts and users with the Discovery tag by typing into the search bar.

Viewing Updates – When someone performs any activity related to your updates, such as commenting on an image, following you, tagging you, or more, you are notified in the "News" tab. You can display your interest in pictures by pressing the heart-shaped icon under the photo ("liking" the photo). For commenting on an image, simply click on the bubble icon and leave your comment.

Adding Photographs on Instagram – Click on the "Share" tab to select pictures from your device's image gallery. If you want to take a new photo and instantly upload it on Instagram, click the "Share" button followed by the camera icon. Click Next once you are done. Instagram doesn't have many editing options except for the standard rotation, adding frames, creating blurring photo effects, brightening photos and other similar features. Filters are quite popular with Instagram users. Scroll through the filters at the bottom of the image to pick the one that best suits your photograph.

Adding a Description for the Image – Enter a description under the "What" field. Adding a short description along with a couple of hashtags will make your post more searchable for users. A location can be added by selecting the "Where" option.

Chapter 6

The Top 14 Instagram Marketing Secrets

1. *Partner With a Worthy Cause Compatible With Your Brand* – Collaborating with noble causes that are congruent with your brand values is a brilliant way to build a community on Instagram. Take SweetGreen, for instance. They are a lunch spot known for their organic and directly-from-farmers sourced ingredients. They've entered into a seamless partnership with FoodCorps that espouses healthy eating choices among children.

SweetGreen posted an image of a little girl digging into a bowl of fresh vegetables, which beautifully aligned with the values of both organizations. It was a well drafted post that successfully raised awareness about healthy eating choices, demonstrated the meaningful partnership between the two brands, and reinforced what SweetGreen stands for. Align your company's or website's values with customers.

2. *Share Your Brand Story* – Few things tug at people's heartstrings like a company story shared personably and compellingly. Use cool, interesting and meaningful images to present your company's fundamental values.

Make top executives appear approachable and human by posting quirky, funny, and interesting posts about them on Instagram. For instance, what are they most likely to do when they aren't working, or something really whacky and fun which people just wouldn't expect from them.

3. *Photo Captions and Contests* – A super way to increase engagement on Instragram is by sharing images of your products/service/niche or something related to your brand, and asking followers to have a blast captioning those images.

Pro tip: Try and hold a photo captioning contest, where you can encourage followers to participate by giving out cool prizes.

4. *Hashtagging Contests* – Hashtagging contests are the newest rage on Instagram. They are a fun and personalized to get users involved in content creation. Ask followers to upload photographs with your unique hashtag. They can then collectively vote for a winner.

Jorg Gory Gray created a nice hashtag contest. They asked visitors to share a photograph with a Jorg Gory Gray timepiece using the #jorgstyle hashtag. Winners were given a free Jorg Gory Gray watch. Great way to build a fun and loyal following? You bet.

5. *Use hashtags* – Hashtags are an important part of Instagram and one of the best ways to wow followers. Connect with your audience by including a couple of unique, meaningful, and interesting hashtags. Don't overdo it or you'll come across as desperate.

Connect using the right emotions and values that are most likely to strike a chord with your target audience.

Make different hashtags for different campaigns to make it easier for you and your followers to keep track of multiple campaigns.

6. *Give Your Followers Some Fame* – Making your followers famous by sharing their photographs on Instagram is a great way to show them some much needed appreciation and win their hearts. Starbucks (which is one of the top three Instagram brands) successfully uses this strategy.

They often give a shout out for to their fans by including the a fan's image with Starbucks's most iconic products. The warm fuzzies feelings are further boosted when they use these images as fun Facebook covers.

Do the fans love it and come back for more? You bet. It is always good to seek permission from your fans before sharing their photographs.

Mention your followers with @username whenever you can, especially when they post pictures with your products. This is a great way to express gratitude and increase your involvement with your audience. Coke does this frequently. They often mention customers who win Instagram photo contests, making them feel super special and fuzzyvalued.

Since Instagram gives now offers you the option of directly embedding images from the network onto your site/blogwebsite or blog, use your customer's' images on your blog, too, to make them feel a part of your brand's loyal community.

7. *Showcase Your Products/Services Creatively* – Be hip, cool, and creative on Instagram. Pilot Pen USA is a superb example of how virtually any company can make it big on Instagram, and not just the ones selling clothes, cakes, and crafts.

Coming back to Pilot Pens, yYou may wonder how a company selling something as boring and uninspiring as pens comes up with attractive Instagram posts.

Well, creative thinking is the only secret sauce here. They post regular photographs of hand created notes using their pens?! And expectedly, their fans love the personal touch and relevance.

8. *Partner With with Other Brands* – Whether you are a one-man blog business or a mid-sized local business, there's always a scope way to forge meaningful relationships with other brands.

Partner up with other similar brands and get them to feature your products, while you post theirs on your Instagram feed. For instance, if you run a local cake shop or jewelry shop, you can get a popular wedding planner to feature your products on their feed, while you recommend their services to your followers. A sure-shot win-win.

9. *Have a Clear Branding Strategy* – Your brand is unique in its personality and in the way it sees the world. Connect your followers with the unique vibe of your brand. Build a link between your business (brand) and your Instagram tribe in a consistent and compellingly visual manner. Get your followers to adore your brand for its awesomeness.

10. *The Infallible Ask Technique* – One of the best ways to engage customers on Instagram (or most social media networks for that matter) is to simply ask. Don't assume oOnce you build an attractive page with a super line up of images, don't assume, that people will swarm like bees and create a buzz about your products/servicesto it on their own.

QQuestions are invitations for discussions and conversations. They may open up many new avenues which you may might not have thought about earlier.

Ask your fans relevant and interesting questions related to your products/ and services. Solicit opinion about a new product. Ask followers for tips or advice related to your industry. Create a unique hashtag and ask customers to share their experiences about your products or services.

For instance, if you run a service related to toddlers such as day care, a toy store, or something similar, you can ask parents to post pictures of their children with a unique hashtag and their number one toddler parenting tip. In this example, parents want to feel a part of a community and establish fruitful relationships with people who are in the same situation as they are. You create that community by being relevant to their needs, building connections, and giving them value.

11. *Build Story Arcs* – Well you've seen people sharing a bunch of attractive yet unrelated pictures together and garnering plenty of attention. Why not create stories out of these images by building a sequence around them? Think of creative story arcs, where each image can be used to take the story ahead. Images can also be posted to present progressions over a period of time. People love stories and actionable images that tell interesting stories.

12. *Experiment Withwith Your Product Images* – Think of new and interesting ways to showcase your products/ and services to your target audience. Use different settings and backgrounds to pique the curiosity of your followers. Create these images especially for Instagram and do not share them on any other social media platform to maintain exclusivity. Creative photography and innovative product shoots add more punch to your profile. There are innumerable ways to do this even with standard products.

For example, salons and spas can post images of exquisite nail art with elegant hand postures or holding objects that complement the color scheme of the nail art. Visually dazzling? You bet. Pose with a violin or guitar to showcase nail art more creatively and unexpectedly.

If you run a beauty blog or beauty store or sell cosmetics, create a collage of various women wearing the same red lipstick to showcase how the shade can flatter different skin tones.

On a visually action-packed and dynamic platform like Instagram, visitors will soon lose interest if you simply keep posting dull and unexciting images of your products/ and services. You need to pump action into them to transform even the blandest products into Instagram superheroes.

13. *Use Videos* – Instagram has a godsent great feature (pardon the exaggeration) that allows users to record tiny video clips going up to 15 seconds. This opens up a whole new way to connect with your audience.

Use the feature to create stellar behind-the-scenes videos for your brand or tell a story about your employees or the company founder for that matter. Use its Instagram's filters innovatively to create stunning animations. You can create several videos and then splice them into something extraordinary.

14. *Avoid Negativity* – This should be self-evident, but given the conversations that happen on Instagram every day, it doesn't appear to be so. Be polite, civil, and professional in your interactions. There's no need to get sucked into dirt if one of the trolls is having a field day on your post. Rather than stopping stooping to their level, simply block them to retain your positivity and sanity.

Keep in mind that not everyone you follow will posts things that you agree with. This isn't reason enough to get agitated and spew venom on a social platform. Again, you can simply unfollow such folks rather than get into a senseless battle of wits.

When others behave badly, it is indeed a superb opportunity to showcase your grace and poise. Be tactful, and courteous, and avoid negative confrontations.

Chapter 7

Cracking the LinkedIn Code

Often treated as the more officious and decorous social media step-child, LinkedIn remained staggeringly untapped for long. Until recently, people did not wise up to its marketing and promotional benefits. From a mere job and resume site, it has now become a powerful platform for forging professional connections and networks.

With over 450 million users, the business networking giant is slated to grow at a monumental pace in coming years.

It is a professional networking media all right. However, that's exactly why it is such a solid and dependable marketing platform. If you know the little known tricks and pro tips, there's nothing stopping you from creating a strong brand using LinkedIn. Here's everything you want to know about this social media superpower.

Customize Your Profile URL

Instead of having a profile URL with a zillion numbers on it, customize it by going to the profile URL option located in the right-hand corner. Your public profile will appear saner and more professional such as http://www.linkedin.com/JohnSmith.

Add a Background Personal Profile Photo

In 2104, LinkedIn finally opened itself up to the cover photo social media phenomenon. This adds a bit more persona and character to your profile. Ensure you pick a profile that's in tandem with the professional social media tone of LinkedIn.

Add a background profile photo by clicking on Profile > Edit Profile (LinkedIn's upper navigation bar) > Add a Background Photo. You can modify an existing background photo by clicking on it and selecting the Edit Background option.

Your cover photo, according to LinkedIn specifications, must be a PNG, GIF or JPG file only (under 8 MG). The ideal resolution is 1400 x 425 pixels.

Add the LinkedIn Badge

Another unique and professionally befitting feature that LinkedIn has is the Profile Badge. Expand your professional connections by displaying this badge (there are many options to pick from) on your blog or website. It links directly to your LinkedIn profile.

Display Work Samples

Well, people are searching you on LinkedIn because they want to see your professional work before associating with you.

Not many know that LinkedIn offers the feature of adding tons of media including videos, graphics, documents, and presentations under the Experience, Summary and Education sections of your profile. Use them to showcase your brilliance.

Add projects and portfolios. Try to add a variety of samples to give potential clients a glimpse of your versatility.

Recommend People

LinkedIn focuses heavily of building business networks and recommending people professionally.

When you recommend people, you find them returning the favor by treating your brand more positively. You not just feel good about endorsing a worthy product and service, but you also attract goodwill for your own brand, lasting professional partnerships, and greater participation.

Join Groups

Groups are one of the best ways to draw traffic to your profile. Join as many relevant groups as you can and contribute regularly. Active participation is key when it comes to being a seamless part of a thriving professional community.

Share interesting and industry-relevant content, initiate thought-provoking discussions, and contribute to existing conversations. This establishes the credibility of your brand, while giving you access to a whole new world of professional connections.

Lasting client-brand relationships and brand promotion is what you should aim for while creating formidable groups. However, don't sell yourself too hard. Focus instead on selling your brilliance and knowledge by creating and sharing top notch content.

When people become a part of specific groups, it shows up on their profile, thus triggering the curiosity of their connections. Additionally, group members can view each other's profiles without actually being connected.

The best way to reach out to potential customers and associates via LinkedIn is by joining as many groups as possible.

When two people are part of one group, the need to be a first degree connection (direct connection of a person rather than the connection of a connection) is eliminated for having a direct conversation.

If you've been on LinkedIn for a month and a member of the group for a minimum of 4 days, LinkedIn lets you send 15 one-on-one messages free to all group members for every group you are a part of.

Getting Endorsed for Your Skills

LinkedIn has a feature that allows your connections to endorse skills listed under the Skills section or even suggest others that you haven't mentioned there. These endorsements are displayed right under the skills mentioned in your profile.

Not every connection is going to endorse your skills, of course. However, since it is easy to endorse someone (simply click on + next to the skill on a profile); connections endorse each other's skills as goodwill gestures.

Ensure your profile is complete and you've listed all skills to make it easier for your connections to endorse them. This definitely boosts your brand's authenticity and credibility.

You can delete endorsements that are inaccurate or plain bizarre. Fire eating, anyone?

Use LinkedIn's Pulse Publishing Platform Optimally

LinkedIn's Pulse publishing platform gives you a brilliant opportunity to showcase your skills by generating authoritative and useful content and sharing it with your connections.

Updating your LinkedIn blog with regular, valuable, and information-rich content can give you great influencer leverage and present yourself as an industry authority, thus boosting your brand credibility. Keep content relevant to your industry, detailed and analytical, and multi-perspective.

You can also syndicate content from your corporate blog to LinkedIn Pulse, thus drawing a larger audience to your blog. To publish an article, select Publish a Post. You can also go to Pulse from the Interests option on the main navigation toolbar.

Select Publish a Post once you are done by clicking the top right corner button on the page.

Make Your Profile More Accessible

When you visit other profiles, allow them to be able to see your profile, too. Go to Settings and click on your profile image. Click Manage > Profile > Privacy Controls > Select What Others See When You've Viewed Their Profile. Check the Your Name and Headline feature.

Use Saved Searches

LinkedIn lets you store a maximum of three people searches and 10 job searches by clicking the Save Search option on the upper right corner. This makes it easy for you to track searches and peruse the information later. Users can get weekly or monthly email reminders when new network users or jobs matching the saved criteria spring up.

Open Profile for More Connections

As discussed earlier, only first degree connections can private message each other. This means you can touch base one-on-one with only those customers who are in the same groups as you.

However, there's a way through which you can send other users messages without being a first degree connection. It is called the Open Profile option, and is only available to premium account members.

If you opt for the Open Profile Network, any user (irrespective of their LinkedIn membership or degree of connection) is available to you for one-on-one messaging.

Send an Open Profile Message by clicking on Send an InMail. You can also hover around the top section of the user's profile section and choose Select an InMail. Premium account holders can simply select Send (user's name) and the messaging button.

Check Out Who's Checking You Out

Just like you want the users of profiles you visit to know about you, you also want to access profiles of users who visit your profile. With the Who's Viewed Your Profile option, accessible within the main navigation in the Profile dropdown, you can view all users who've visited your profile.

Also, LinkedIn has gone a step further and made it even more comprehensive by including a feature where you can actually view how your profile stacks up against your connections' profile views. This opens up a whole new list of potential clients and business associates.

Optimize Your Profile for Search Engines

Optimize your profile by including key search terms and words that are normally used to describe your profession. The more specific you are, the more likely you are to be found while people search for those terms on search engines. Include keywords in multiple profile sections, including the profile headline and summary.

LinkedIn allows you to add links to websites within your profile. A neat little tip is to retain links to your other social media pages but change the link text (the clickable words that take visitors to another page) to include more impactful keywords and phrases related to your business.

For instance, your Twitter profile link can read as C++Coder Twitter Profile. This captures the gist of your profile and makes it more optimized for search engines.

Use the Advanced Search Option

LinkedIn's Advanced Search option offers a much more focused search experience. For example, maybe you want to know if you are connected to someone who is employed by a specific organization. You simply need to mention the company name and then use the relationships filter for checking if you have any connections with the specific user.

Cross-Promote by Sharing LinkedIn Updates on Twitter

Though you can't automatically publish your tweets on LinkedIn, the reverse can be achieved with startling results by adding your Twitter profile to LinkedIn. If you want your Twitter followers to be able to access your LinkedIn updates, syndicate update posts by choosing the Public + Twitter feature under the Share With dropdown option within the update composer.

New and Existing Connections

The Connections tab in the top navigation offers plenty of features to grow your connections and expand your professional network. Click on Add Connections from the dropdown option to extract contacts using your email accounts and get suggestions and recommendations for more connections. You can connect with others from your university using the Find Alumni function.

Keep in Touch is another unique feature that lets you stay in touch with existing connections, track your communications with them, get notified when they change jobs, and gives birthday reminders.

Email LinkedIn Groups

Can LinkedIn groups be used to generate leads? Yes, of course. One of the biggest advantages of managing a group is that you can send out messages to each group member (a maximum of once per week). These messages are sent as LinkedIn announcements straight into the inboxes of members, if they enable the 'messages from groups' from their settings.

If you build a thriving group that is packed with insightful discussions, you are tapping into a robust group of targeted customers and associates. You can generate plenty of leads by directing group users to your LinkedIn profile and ultimately to your blog or other social media pages.

Maintain top notch group etiquette by keeping discussions professional and relevant. Rather than focusing on promoting your product, focus on adding more value within the topic so other users can benefit from it.

Once they see you contributing meaningfully to the group, they will automatically take greater interest in your profile, and they will automatically be more receptive to your messages.

Add Weight to Your Profile

If you are a fairly new networker or blog owner or business founder, and don't know how to add more weight to your profile, think again! There's plenty that you can put in there to pack more panache into your profile.

It can be anything from knowledge of foreign languages to special volunteer experience to any special projects you've worked on. Since you can add media to your profile too, how about an interesting introductory video that demonstrates your skills?

To add media to your file, Click Edit Profile and select the square icon under Summary and Educations sections. Click to upload media files.

Conclusion

Thank you for downloading *Social Media Marketing: A Beginner's Guide to Dominating the Market with Social Media Marketing.*

I hope the book helped you gain invaluable insights about the basics of social media marketing, as well as its little-known, actionable, and practical tips. Using the simple yet effective nuggets of information given in the book, you can come up with your own creative ways to build a powerful online presence for your brand.

The next step is to convert your learning into action. Create a comprehensive social media marketing plan using the expert hints described in the book and implement it confidently. Patience and persistence are the keys to creating stellar social media brands. Take action now and keep going until you see the desired results! You will be surprised!

Social Media Marketing

Strategies to Capture and Engage Your
Audience While Quickly Building Authority

Chapter 1

What is Social Media Marketing

Have you ever performed on stage? If you have, you know that the performer has to go out there and perform to the absolute best of their ability. They must showcase their brilliant talents for applause. They must win the hearts of an eager audience.

Think of your virtual stage now. The audience is waiting to be enthralled and entertained. A few dull moments and they are gone. They want to be engaged, informed, entertained, and inspired. Your social media pages are a virtual stage.

Those social media pages are dynamic, evolving, and rapidly growing audience engagement channels that help you captivate readers or potential customers. Your readers come out feeling awestruck or bored depending on your performance and how you manage to strike a chord in them.

Think of social media as a house dinner, where along with a group of family, friends, and colleagues, there will also be a few uninvited guests who tagged along with someone.

These are the skeptics, trolls, and naysayers who attend gatherings without invitation and probably never want to leave (we've all had that one painful, uninvited guest). Others may have arrived by invitation and still not behaved themselves. They may try to hog the party's attention by being obnoxious, rude, or plain egocentric.

This is exactly what happens in your virtual house party. There are all kinds of audience members, some truly aggressive and attention-grabbing, others plain fools, and still others absolutely open and willing to contribute to a meaningful conversation started by the host.

You can also look at social media marketing like dating. Would you ask your date to marry you on the first date itself? Chances are they'd freak out and never see you again.

Can you sell to your customer immediately after introducing your products and services or brand to him? Yes. But would that make him a loyal and repeat buyer? Probably not. He may buy just to shut you up and get rid of you, but that won't help transform him into a lifelong buyer.

How can you get someone you really liked on a first date to marry you? You make an effort to understand the person. You try to gather as much information about their likes, dislikes, aspirations, desires, goals, and so on so that you can impress them.

You then go about sweeping them off their feet before making it impossible for them to refuse your marriage proposal. You electrify and impress them to such an extent that they just can't say no to you.

Social media marketing is just like the wooing and relationship development phase before you can make your customers say "I do" to buying your products or services. It's about building such strong relationships that potential buyers find it hard to say no to you.

Social media is all about building relationships through engagement and establishing authority. It is about growing your followers and drawing traffic to your website with various resourceful customer engagement strategies. Social media is about building your brand and credibility to create heightened customer loyalty.

It's about giving your audience irresistible value in the form of blogs, images, instructional how-to's, infographics, and more. It is about making their lives simpler and more productive by offering ideas and resources.

Social media bridges the gap between introducing yourself to potential customers and turning them into brand-loyal evangelists. It awards you a platform for building trust by forging strong connections with customers.

It gives you the opportunity to establish the credibility and authority of your brand before people can trust you enough to buy from you.

Let us get back to the dating analogy. If you are simply listing the benefits or features of your products and services with a call to action link under it, essentially you telling your target audience, we may not know each other but I still presume you will not say no to me.

You are asking your poor leads to get serious way too soon, without investing in the 'courtship' phase.

Why do you expect them to commit to buying immediately after meeting you? Just cool it a bit. Why don't you give them a chance to get to know you? Why not throw in some free information or an eBook related to your products or services?

It vouches for your authority in a particular domain, while helping your leads develop a warm feeling for the brand. You keep notching up the commitment levels with webinars, case studies, data, demo videos, FAQs, and so on. You work to take leads or prospective customers through a purchase cycle by creating awareness through engagement, followed by an evaluation of their wants.

The next stage is the purchase stage, followed by continuously engaging loyal customers. You don't stop wooing the special someone you married, do you? (Well, some people might, but I can't vouch for the success of their marriages).

You still keep doing things for your spouse lest they dump you and get married to someone else. You have to keep your existing customers 'married' to you, too. There are far too many other firms that have designs on them and will be only happy to 'break your marriage' and acquire them.

Social media is a brilliant way to keep your customers from straying. Through continuous engagement and value addition, you can ensure your customers have no reason to leave.

Pamper them with information, entertainment, and inspiration that drives their daily life, and you'll have little trouble keeping your customers. Creating meaningful engagement is key.

What are the most compelling hopes, fears, and dreams of your target audience? What are the fundamental problems in their lives? How can you solve those problems and make their lives slightly easier? What can you do to add more value to their lives?

If you can work all this out, then your target audience will want to be "married" to your products or services. They need a reason to base their purchasing decisions on. The reason can be either emotions or logic or a combination of both.

If you can appeal to their emotions or logic through an astute brand building strategy on social media, they'll find a compelling reason to purchase from you. The more popular your content or value addition gets, the higher will be the number of people eager to buy from you.

Social media is excellent from the perspective of creating positive social signals for your brand. You know how a beauty or prom queen contest works, right? The higher number of votes you receive, the better are your chances of being crowned the prom queen. Likewise, the number of committee member votes decides who will be the next club secretary. This is exactly how social signals work to rank you on organic searches.

When your content is magnificent, it gets the nod of approval from your social media audience. People want to share it and include links to it on their pages. The internet users vote for your content. Every like, share, or link back to your content is a vote in your favor.

Because search engines always strive to offer their best to their audience, they want to place content that's garnered plenty of votes and endorsements in the form of social signals (such as liking, commenting, sharing, and so on) high on search results.

This naturally enhances your search engine page rankings and shows up in the top results for a term related to your products or services.

Creating top notch content not just offers value to your audience, but also fulfills the purpose of establishing you as an expert in your industry. It helps you come across as a social influencer who can wield considerable force over people's purchasing decisions.

People love to expose themselves and their social circle to updated, analytical, meaningful, and thought-provoking content.

Always keep in mind that people enjoy sharing content that makes them come across as intelligent, aware, and well-read in front of their family and peer group.

By creating powerful content, you are giving them something valuable to share with their followers. You are giving them the opportunity to flaunt their intelligence and feel special within their group.

People are always seeking acceptance and a validation from others. Giving them something on a platter that will help them gain social currency (or acceptance and validation) from peers is a foolproof way to win their vote of confidence.

People don't buy from robots or machines, so sounding like one is a surefire way to business disaster. People buy from other people. They buy from humanized brands that they feel a sense of belonging with. They buy from brands whose values and visions are in tandem with theirs.

Assume you had a salesman come to you and conduct a long monologue about the merits of his product. This monologue is then followed with a request that you purchase the product. What is your reaction? Are you inspired and engaged? Do you identify with the brand enough to commit to a purchase? Definitely not.

Now take a scenario where you meet a salesman who is not too focused on selling his product and wants to simply engage in a conversation to understand your wants. He just wants to have a conversation with you, irrespective of whether you buy from him or not.

You start talking, and he pays attention. You share your thoughts and ideas about industry trends, and he adds to it with his own expertise. Sometimes, he launches a topic and you give your unique take on it.

What ensues is a meaningful, fruitful, and mutually beneficial conversation where each of you has learned something about the other.

Now, you have established a sound rapport with the salesman. This makes you comfortable enough to check out his products and services. You discover, much to your enthusiasm, that he is showing you only those products that fulfill your needs, which you spoke about during your conversation.

You discover that the products and services absolutely fit your requirements and you are glad to go ahead with the purchase. Isn't this what social media marketing is all about? It is 80% building relationships and authority through engagement, and only 20% selling.

Your brand is a person. A unique person with its own set of values and attributes. People will buy only when they like your brand and feel a sense of belonging with it. The brand will come across as desirable only when you convey its attributes in an unusual and interesting manner.

Make your brand desirable and irresistible by engaging your audience. Get people to buy your vision by establishing authority before they actually buy your products or services.

Building a solid social media presence and developing authority is similar to jogging. If you start doing it for 30 minutes each day consistently, you begin to see results over time.

You can't jog for an entire day and expect to see results at the end of the day. Social media marketing is not an overnight process. It is about building and nurturing a following, much like creating a flourishing garden.

You need patience, persistence, discipline, resourcefulness and dogged determination to succeed. The results, just like jogging, may not be immediate, but over a period of time, you find yourself more active, flexible, energetic, and lighter.

Social media marketing is a long-term and persistent effort unlike short sprints of extreme activity. It isn't focused on short-term gain; it isn't about making a few quick sales. The platform is for forging life-long relationship bonds with your customers.

It is about seeding, watering, weeding, and eventually yielding returns. It is about nurturing a garden of trust, relationships, and credibility before reaping from it. It isn't about saying "buy this or that from us." Rather, it helps customers make smart buying choices that suit their requirements.

You don't sell on social media, you help your customers buy. There is an ocean of difference between the two and each requires drastically different thought processes. Whereas salesmen will focus on selling, relationship builders will focus on understanding what the customer wants so that they can help them make purchasing decisions.

If you simply use your social media platforms for selling, the returns will most likely be short-term. However, if you nurture a powerful and loyal community of buyers, you are on your way to building a highly profitable venture.

Reach out to prospective customers through focused groups and communities. Network with clients and business associates by posting quality content that wins approval. Share content that offers an important purpose or successfully solves the problem of your carefully built social community.

Why Social Media Marketing?

1. *Social media helps you build influencer authority*. It offers you several cutting-edge tools for content creation such blog posts, latest updates, breaking news, opinion polls, analytical pieces, reviews, images, and videos.

Creating original, unique and sharp content positions you as an authority in your niche. It convinces your audience that you know exactly what you are saying.
If you consistently offer valuable content over a period of time, customers are more likely to sit up and take note of your recommendations. Once they trust your opinion, they will be only too happy to buy from you.

As you keep gaining more and more followers, your influence in an industry grows. A higher number of followers start sharing your content, tagging you and talking about you, which makes your brand come across as highly authoritative. Establishing your influence in a domain also provides you with the opportunity of connecting with other industry experts for better reach and exposure.

Imagine creating a powerful blog post that is shared by a leading industry authority who has thousands of followers on their profile. Imagine the reach, exposure, and impact of your post—it would be incredible.

The more useful your posts the wider your influencer network, the higher your content shares will be. Social media gives you the opportunity to reach out to and connect with other industry influencers.

This helps you create a solid content synergy and sharing strategy to widen your reach. Few other marketing channels will give you the benefits of collaboration and mutually beneficial partnerships as much as social media.

2. *Social media boosts your search engine optimization.* Social media marketing is about garnering social signals in the form of engagement and interaction with your audience.

Search engines view different types of engagement such as likes, comments, re-tweets, repins, etc. as an endorsement of your authority, thus placing you higher on search engine rankings when people search for products, services, or information related to your industry.

When your content is shared on social media, users will invariably click on links to check out your blog or company website. Now, imagine you don't have a social media presence—your content will only be accessed by users who are already familiar with your products or services or by those who stumble upon it through search engines by using the relevant keywords. It does not make your content reachable to new users, which social sharing does.

Social media distributes your content all across the web to give a lot of new and potential customers the chance to come across your products or services.

3. *Social media marketing helps you build a platform for great customer experience.* Imagine life before the advent of social media. How would you draw the attention of a company to a faulty product? Or advice about using the product? Most likely via a "contact us" form on their website or an email explaining the nature of your query.

It would take hours or sometimes a couple of days for company representatives to check their mails and respond to you. By then, you were already frustrated and stopped using the product.

Social media has made speedy and efficient service a reality. It has ensured better customer experience by enabling quick resolution of queries. Social media has helped make brands accountable for their products and services on a public platform.

If you are not happy about a product or service, all you need to do is tweet your complaint on Twitter by tagging the brand. Then thousands of their followers will be able to view your complaint.

What do you think companies do in this case? They quickly get to work and focus on resolving the customer's queries so that it doesn't negatively impact the buying decisions of thousands of potential customers. Doesn't this translate into ace customer experience?

Most of your existing customers expect you as a responsible brand to have a social media presence. More than 67 percent of consumers utilize social media for quick customer service.

In a competitive business world where companies are hoping to lure each other's customers, you can lose in a big way if you do not have a solid social media presence to take care of customer service issues.

Customers today expect nothing short of speedy, efficient and 24/7 customer support. They want a fast resolution to their queries. According to an Aberdeen Group study, companies that offer social media customer service witness much higher annual financial gains than firms without a social media customer service presence.

4. *Social media enhances brand recognition.* This should be no-brainer. Imagine Brand A and Brand B. Brand A has

a powerful social media presence. It is constantly engaging with customers by sharing important industry updates, triggering meaningful debates, and creating valuable content. Brand A has a clear, consistent, and interesting voice that you can identify with.

Through a clever content strategy, Brand A is making itself more desirable and accessible to potential customers and more recognizable and dependable for existing customers. You constantly see the name of Brand A being mentioned in your feed on multiple social media networks.

In contrast, Brand B has hardly any social media presence. Maybe an account or two on some popular social networks, where it fails to engage its audience and mostly posts links to sales pages. If given a choice, which brand would you purchase from?

Obviously the one that enjoys greater exposure because it is more popular, interesting, and customer-centric. Brand A's social media presence shows you that the brand cares about its customers enough to engage with them.

Don't you like a brand that shows some love to its customers? Wouldn't you like to return the love by buying from Brand A? Brands that enjoy greater visibility and more exposure score when it comes to familiarity.

Consumers instantly identify Brand A's products or services when it comes to making buying decisions. The brand name immediately resonates with customers because they've been exposed to it several times on social media.

5. *Social media offers higher conversion opportunities.* Each post you create or share on the social media is a chance to convert your audience into buyers.

Your follower pool consists of a mix of old, new, and prospective customers, and you can interact with and target everyone with your blog posts, videos, images, and comments.
Every piece of content provides an opportunity for your audience to react. This reaction leads to interaction and conversation, which can ultimately lead to conversion.

Of course, not every conversation or reaction is going to result in conversion. However, every positive and optimistic interaction boosts the likelihood of a conversion. If you have a huge following, even with low click-through rates, you can rake decent profits through the sheer number of conversion opportunities.

If you are omnipresent on the internet, your customers find it simpler to search you out and connect with you. This leads to a far greater engagement to remind them about your existence. You stay at the top of their awareness.

Consumer retention and loyalty is bound to increase when you are instantly interacting with customers, while offering them stellar support and value-added content.

6. *Social media marketing cuts your marketing and promotion budget and time while still delivering brilliant results.* A rather illuminating Hubspot survey revealed that 84% of marketers discovered that spending about 6 hours a week on social media was enough to boost their traffic generation efforts.

About an hour a day spent on content development, syndication, and sharing is enough to help you reap increased traffic results.

Presume you have a few hundred followers initially and you create spectacular content that absolutely adds value to their lives. A handful of them share the content, comment on it, like it, retweet it, or perform other similar actions. Now your message has reached all the followers of each of those followers who shared your message.

Those followers in turn are impressed enough to share your message with thousands of their followers. See the exponential growth? And what did it cost you to create the post? Probably a few hours and some helpful tools.

The world is your oyster on social media. You can target a large number of people, located anywhere on the planet, with a miniscule budget. Even paid advertisements and promotions offered by different social networks help you effectively target customers at prices lower than those of traditional advertising channels.

A Facebook local paid advertising service will probably cost you much less than hiring a billboard or running a commercial on your local satellite network, while also offering you a more targeted audience base.

Even the potential losses in social media are minimal compared to traditional marketing and promotional channels. Practically speaking, what do you stand to lose if a social media campaign doesn't take off too well in the first instance? Some time and effort probably? Or negligible social media advertising revenue at the most?

7. *Social media offers you better customer insights.* Social listening is so vital when you want your target audience to take action in your favor. Don't you want to gain vital insights into the behavior, demographics, fears, goals, and driving forces of your audience? Don't you want to know what motivates them to take action or what their most basic requirements are?

Well, social media helps you do exactly that. It helps you gain interesting insights about audience behavior, which acts as cues to design brilliant marketing messages. Once you know what drives, excites, and scares your audience, it is easier to create content that resonates with them.

For instance, if you are about to launch a new product, you can post some information about it and see your audience reaction in the form of comments or shares. You can also gauge what type of content appeals most to them by measuring audience engagement. There is greater flexibility to finetune your content and products according to audience feedback or insights.

This can give you a solid edge over competitors who haven't yet woken up to the benefits of social media marketing. You don't need much time to create a social media profile and a few engaging posts, compared to several other marketing mediums.

Social media gives you greater scope for testing different promotional campaigns and strategies before understanding where your audience is and which channel yields maximum results.

Geo-targeting is another great way to reach out to a targeted audience based on their location. This works brilliantly for local businesses that are trying to create a social presence for themselves. For instance, you can use Hootsuite to send Twitter messages only to followers in a specific location.

Both Facebook and Twitter feature promotional tools that allow business owners to target customers in a particular region. This gives you a more incisively targeted local audience who may be interested in your products and services.

8. *Social media allows you to evaluate competitor strategy.* Social media monitoring allows you to gain valuable insights about competitors to up your game.

Greater competitor insights allow businesses to make strategic promotional decisions.

For example, Hootsuite allows you to create searches where you can constantly monitor keywords related to your industry, while keeping a close eye on the competition.

Based on these valuable revelations, you can incorporate everything they are missing or offer improved products and services or better customer service.

Chapter 2

Facebook for Building Authority

Facebook has close to 2 billion active worldwide users. There are about 300 million photographs uploaded in a single day, while 20 minutes is the average time spent on it per visit. There are 293,000 posts and 510 comments posted on it every minute.

Can you afford to leave Facebook out of your online marketing and authority building campaign? Most certainly not. Here are some expert tips to help you gain greater mileage from Facebook to boost visibility, authority, and brand-building efforts.

Opt for Quality over Quantity

Spend time drafting and posting a couple of quality posts a day rather than littering your followers' walls with meaningless updates. Avoid using scattershot updates that fly everywhere without having any relevance to your audience. Dan and Alison Zarrella's The Facebook Marketing Book says posting once a day gives you optimal value.

Keep your updates sticky and conversation triggering. Stay away from writing thesis length posts. No one has the time to read them on Facebook. Include an interesting punchline or update and link to your blog, where readers who are interested in reading further can be diverted. You can also import your blog to Facebook notes if you wish to create more elaborate updates.

Be judicious about what you post if you want people to sit up and take note. You don't have to post each time you clean your backyard or have your breakfast. Link to stories that are sexy, hilarious, remarkably unique, or newsworthy.

Always include a picture to go with the tone of your posts. The idea is to stoke engagement. Post interesting things that will get people talking.

Use the Appropriate Channels

The tools that you use to convey your message not just help you build authority in the eyes of your audience, but also helps you build authority in the eyes of Facebook itself. The social media network is constantly monitoring and rating your content to gauge your influence, though it isn't likely that they will reveal their exact algorithms.

Use videos (more than 150 years of YouTube video is consumed on Facebook alone each day) to increase your influencer quotient by embedding the video or posting a YouTube link of the video on your wall.

Several Facebook marketing experts believe the social network's algorithms offer extra juice to geo location updates. Given the frenzy of our smart phone driven society that thrives on minute-by-minute updates, this seems reasonable enough.

Use Facebook Places rather than Foursquare of Gowalla. It has far more clout on the network. This will also help you reach local customers and businesses, and establish a strong media presence within the local buying community.

Another way to up your Facebook juice is to upload and tag images on your page. More than 4 billion images are uploaded on the social media network, making it the world's largest photo sharing site. Use high-quality, clear, and appropriate images that evoke the desired response from your audience.

Ensure you go through copyright laws before simply stealing images from other sources. As far as possible, use your own images photo albums. Tagging is a good way to boost exposure, however ensure you tag the right people who are actually associated with or interested in the image.

Though you'd like to believe otherwise, Facebook doesn't just revolve around your posts. There are lots of other interesting and exciting things that can be shared with your followers. Remember, however, to add your own unique take, insightful comment, or provocative observations to the content.

Use Facebook's comments option to build authority by leaving value-added, insightful, and well-researched comments on others' posts. It boosts your overall exposure. Remember to always contribute meaningfully to the conversation. Attempt to solve people's problems or give your unique views on important, topical discussions.

Reveal your industry expertise by quoting specific numbers or little-known facts. Authority will not be built overnight. You have to keep at it until you start seeing small, positive results, and take it from there.

"Liking" other posts is another good way to gain traction on Facebook. Use it liberally for topical discussions or news items or comments you appreciate on other pages. This doesn't mean that you will hog the limelight in other users' news feeds, but it will establish your supportive and encouraging reputation. People will appreciate you endorsing and participating on their pages, and they will most likely return the favor when they come across something interesting on your wall.

Also, acknowledge the comments of users who comment on your posts with a like or reply. This sends them an instant notification, which can then draw them back to the discussion thread. Replying to their comments makes your audience feel more involved and engaged, thus keeping the conversation alive and thriving.

Ask Questions

Take a moment to scan through some popular competitor pages on Facebook. Which are the posts that garner maximum comments or interactions? Those are the posts where someone asks a question or important questions are raised. Question posts elicit maximum response. Why do you think this is?

Showing off is a natural human tendency. Everyone wants to flaunt their intellectual radiance by chiming in with their two cents of advice or their own solution. People are always on the lookout for opportunities where they can pitch in to reveal their intelligence.

Soliciting advice through thought-provoking and relevant questions is a foolproof way to get people involved. When you post regular updates, you aren't urging them to respond, but with questions, you are giving them pointers on how you want them to interact. You are directly asking for answers. They know exactly what they are supposed to do and will happily pitch in.

Include a potpourri of questions. Some questions could be related to a personal issue. For instance, if you run a business related to young children, you can take personal questions from readers about issues they are facing while bringing up their child and put forth the question to your audience, asking them to come up with solutions.

You could also ask them for professional suggestions, such as changing the interface or design of your blog. Get your imagination soaring and ask fill-in-the-blanks questions such as "This is a good time for..." or "It is never too late to..." Let your followers complete the line with their own witty and whacky responses.

Grow Your Network

New pages will have a tough time getting their statuses to appear in their followers' and fans' newsfeeds. Focus on building your initial 500 followers and keep them engaged in a genuine, non-spammy, and positive manner. This will boost the likelihood of your updates appearing on their feed more than having an avalanche of followers with minimal exposure.

Once visibility is bumped up, you can focus on building a larger network of followers to gain more sway. Ensure that in the beginning, your Show Posts From under the Menu options is set to "All of Your Friends and Pages" and not "Friends and Pages You Interact with Most."

Here are some of the best insider tips to boost your Facebook following.

1. *Network with Other Page Administrators and Managers*
One of the most solid strategies to widen your reach and gain authority is by networking with page administrators and social media managers who manage pages similar to yours. This helps in cross promotion and boosts your reach. For example, let's say you run a local café. You can easily tie up with a popular ice cream shop in the neighborhood, which has a clientele similar to yours. Do a little bit of cross promotion by sharing each other's status updates occasionally.

There are other value-added collaborations you can undertake, such as jointly hosting a webinar to gain more audience visibility. If you run a personal chef or catering business, you can tie up with a local grocery store and develop interesting, cooking-based webinars. Get resourceful and think of how you can forge meaningful connections to boost visibility for each company.

Creating promotional swaps is a great way to build a targeted following. You can start by looking for about 20-40 pages of products or services which are complementary to yours.

You will most likely share your target audience and have more or less the same page statistics (the same number of fans, for example). Once the list is ready, reach out to the page managers by providing some background about yourself and/or your page engagement statistics (likes, shares, etc.).

Make an offer to include their business page is one of your posts if they agree to return the favor. Do not forget to measure results so you know which partners are beneficial to associate with in future.

2. *Share Original Content*

Try to come up with new ways to present original content. How about a screenshot of a hot tip that is immensely valuable to your target audience? Or an interesting and relevant info graphic? Include original and unique photo presentation as part of your content strategy.

Other ideas are "behind the scenes" images that show what a typical business day is like. You can also post images and ask users to cleverly caption them. Many Facebook influencers love adding inspirational quotes and thought-provoking statements to photographs to attract likes and shares. Label your original photos with the name of your blog or organization.

Another cool authority-building strategy is to post content that is guaranteed to be distributed by your audience. How do you achieve this? It is absolutely simple. Just go to Buzzsumo, which has a list of the most shared content for any given niche.

Enter keywords related to your topic and pull out a list of social media's most shared content. Share these content pieces to gain more traction. Make sure to add your own unique comments while sharing these trending pieces.

3. *Tag Company Pages on Your Personal Profile*
Make it easy for your personal contacts to like your business page by tagging it on your personal profile occasionally. Rather than sharing status updates from the page, tag your business page by selecting the option from the drop-down menu.

The page can be instantly liked from your post itself of people hover the mouse on your tagged page name. This makes it easier for your friends to endorse your business pages, thus boosting your visibility.

Pages, especially the new ones, are not easily spotted in the news feed. This is a neat trick to increase your following and widen your exposure.

4. *Do Not Forget to Link to Your Page from Your Profile*
This should really be a no-brainer, yet plenty of business owners fail to cash in on it. Make it simple for people who are going through your personal profile to locate your business pages by adding them to your profile.

If you do not list where you work, a weird looking ghost-community page is created on your profile rather than a link to your actual business page. In the absence of your business page, people actually start liking the community page (with a suitcase icon) over your real business page. What you need to do is simply delete the community page in your Work and Education section by clicking Edit in your profile's About option. Add your original business page.

5. *Run Contests*

Running contests is a great way to build a loyal and interested audience community. It will help you gain several likes, increase your exposure, and lead to greater engagement from existing fans. Of course, running a contest will require a little investment but the bang for your buck in the form of increased followers and fans makes this a worthy proposition.

Running contests allows you not only to gain more followers but also to promote your products and services in an interesting manner. You can invite people on your mailing list to your Facebook page by sending out contest alert flyers. Include criteria such as liking your page or sharing the post by tagging a few friends as mandatory for participating in the contest.

For instance, if you run a food-related business, list a few ingredients and ask people to come up with original recipes using those ingredients. This is a fun way to gain exposure for products and services, too. You are the winner all the way!

Another popular strategy to gain more exposure used by a lot of companies includes using interesting, funny, and evocative images while asking fans to tag people they think of when they see the image. For example, if the image says something interesting about books or book lovers, ask your fans to tag the bookworms in their friends list in the comments section.

Similarly, if it is a funny meme that says, "I would rather die eating than dieting," ask your fans to tag their food-loving friends. You can then pick a winner from amongst the fans who have commented on the post.

6. *Conduct Interesting Question and Answer Sessions*
This has become a breeze after Facebook launched the reply option. Invite other influencers and industry authorities to answer questions raised by your audience. Responding experts can answer queries in real time, thus making the sessions more interactive and timely.

Promote the session well in advance through status updates and by creating a Facebook event. You will make it simpler for users to invite friends and share information about the upcoming session.

Begin by sending out a well-drafted request to an authority in your industry. Start your mail by appreciating their blog or business and informing them why you would like to have them onboard.

Make a virtual event flyer your Facebook cover photo or profile page for a few days. Include an image of your guest (with permission of course) with details about the event. Promote your event on other social media channels along with related Facebook groups (ask permission before posting on other groups). Send promotional notes to your email subscribers.

7. *Create Facebook Groups*

Creating Facebook groups is a great way to grow your organic reach and gain authority. Groups are known to enjoy greater organic exposure than business pages. When people join groups, group members are informed when new posts are uploaded.

Other benefits include easy file sharing and tagging members to draw them into a conversation. The interaction with users will be carried out through your personal profile, though you can keep discussions related to your business or blog or industry.

For instance, if you run an SEO marketing agency, you can create a general SEO marketing related group where members can hop in and ask queries related to search engine optimization. You or your employees can then address these questions with an expert's flair.

Once users discover value in your answers, they will most likely click on the names of people offering them useful suggestions, which will then translate into exposure for your business pages. The next time these folks want to engage the services of an SEO agency, guess where they'll go?

Ensure you keep the momentum of the group alive by posting regularly, sharing important, industry-relevant updates (while asking members to share their opinion on the same), and posing questions. Channel engagement by sharing value adding content from other pages.

8. *Add Your Facebook Profile in Your Email Signature and Forum Profile*

Add your Facebook profile link within your email signature to ensure every email you send out becomes an opportunity to gain a fan for your business page. People will also get to learn more about you and your business. Include these links when you are creating profiles on industry related forums and discussion boards.

People who are enamored with your contribution to the group in the form of insightful comments or new posts will most likely check out your profile and follow your social media pages and profiles.

Since these forums are so industry specific, you will be attracting a laser-targeted audience. This is also helps you establish authority in your domain.

Chapter 3

Being the Ultimate Twitter Authority

Twitter has an estimated 313 million users currently, with the visitors tally reaching 120 million per month. This clearly indicates that you are sending a lot of money your competitor's way if you do not have a strong Twitter presence. Here are some easy yet effective Twitter authority-building strategies.

Hop on the Popular Content Bandwagon

Ride the content bandwagon by finding Twitter's most popular content (use Buzzsumo) and including it in your content sharing schedule (using Hootsuite).

Why do you want to reinvent the wheel when something is already working so magnificently well? Sprinkle your own stroke of genius by adding a powerful comment or tagline while sharing popular content.

People will most likely retweet this content, which will give you exposure among their followers. Even if only a handful of followers retweet your post, you can still imagine the visibility your brand will attract. Ensure you follow the big guns in your industry to simply tweet what these guys are tweeting.

Network, Network, Network

Avoid networking within your niche until you have about 20 published posts. Find influential people in your industry using FollowerWonk. All you need to do is load the updates of these influencers and click on the star icon adjacent to their most shared content.

Look for profiles that are being followed by more accounts than they follow. Check for keywords related to your industry by scanning the bios and profile descriptions. Go on their updates and save their best posts using the "like" option. You can also save your likes by conducting a search using industry relevant hashtags.

When you like someone's tweets, it features on the user's notification. This helps you grab their attention and gives them an opportunity to check out your profile. They will most likely follow you if they find your tweets interesting.

You can calculate a rough estimate of 50 follows for every 500 likes sent across.

The reason you should employ this strategy over simply following people and expecting them to follow you back (which is what a lot of novices do) is that the latter impacts your follower ratio. The higher your follower ratio, the more you are likely to be viewed as an authority in your domain.

It demonstrates that people aren't simply following you because you follow them but because you have great content that offers value to them. By saving your likes, people are following you on the merit of your content and not merely to return a favor. This boosts your authority and credibility.

Retweet influencer content by tagging them in your tweets. Whenever you tag the person, it shows up in their notifications. If an industry influencer constantly sees you supporting them by sharing their content, they will most likely get familiar with you and be open to networking with you.

Be strategic and pick the right people who are related to your industry. Focus on building a targeted following of highly interested and interactive followers over simply building a mass following of people who do not care about your niche. There's no value in blindly building followers.

Create Relevant Hashtag Campaigns

Creating meaningful and relevant hashtags not only makes it simple to track your campaigns but also encourages greater audience interaction. Create and share a unique, thoughtful, and interesting hashtag to inspire your audience community. Hashtags are a blatant call to action; hence they are capable of drawing more audience engagement.

Take, for instance, Subway's #SaveLunchBreak. It encouraged their followers to avoid skipping their lunch break and instead consume healthy food. It also invigorated people to share how they were enjoying their afternoon meals.

Hashtags create a sense of community. They help forge a strong brand-customer connection by increasing a sense of belonging and helping people feel like part of a single hashtag community.

Create topical and relevant hashtags periodically to engage your audience, boost the community feeling, and build authority.

Before launching a hashtag campaign, decide what you want to achieve with it. What is your primary objective for creating the campaign? Brainstorm to come up with campaign ideas that will resonate with your audience and are relevant to them.

Research what they are constantly talking about to come up with creative, memorable, and identifiable hashtags.

Ask Questions Using Twitter Polls

A fairly recent addition, Twitter Polls gives you the opportunity to obtain feedback from your audience by asking questions in a poll format. To create a poll, go to your tweet editor and select the poll icon. Draft your question and add a maximum of four choices. You can also set the timeframe for which you want the poll to be active (maximum 7 days).

Use this feature to engage your following and build authority. Raise topical, relevant, and thought-provoking questions. Obtain feedback from your audience by asking them to vote for your best blog post, so you know what content to create in future.

Ask for opinions, feedback, something fun, burning issues, or business-related suggestions. Your audience will also appreciate the fact that their opinion is seriously considered.

Keep it Shorter than Short

Yes, there is already a strict character limitation on Twitter that doesn't allow you to go beyond 140 characters. However, shorter tweets of around 110 characters enjoy 17% greater engagement.

The reason behind this phenomenon is that leaving some room in your tweet makes it much simpler for people to add their own take while re-tweeting.

If you utilize the entire 140 characters, those who want to retweet it have to do a bit of editing. And we all know how lazy people can be. Tweets that need editing obviously do not get as many retweets as tweets that can be quickly shared by adding a comment. The ideal tweet is between 80 and 110 characters.

Post Links to Content that Solves Problems

People quickly lap up content that solves a desperate problem. A surefire way to garner engagement and build authority is by posting links to problem-solving content. Scour the web for well-researched and well-written content that rates well when it comes to addressing a pressing issue for your target audience.

Whole Foods has mastered this strategy. They are constantly sharing handy preparation and cooking tips with their followers, while also regularly tweeting seasonal special recipes, eating right advice, and recommendations for top cookbooks.

It isn't tough to determine what your target audience is after. A quick scan through their profiles will give you an idea about their likes and major influences. Select an issue that's common to most followers.

For instance, if you are a family lawyer and have a business following of people who are in the midst of relationship troubles, you can link to a comprehensive article about how to talk to your child about your divorce or how to handle an abusive relationship.

Your followers will appreciate the fact that you are taking the trouble to add more value to their lives by solving their issues.

Avoid Lifestyle Tweets

Unless you're Kim Kardashian, avoid tweeting about your holidays on exotic locales and the fancy breakfast you enjoyed. While your personal profile can have these tweets, your business or brand profile cannot.

Twitter is more suitable as professional marketing network than a personal lifestyle journal. It's all right to be real, but avoid being trivial. Dan Zarrella put together a list of Twitter's 20 least engaging words. No prizes for guessing that words which topped the list, which included "home," "watching," and the like. Spare your followers from personal action tweets if you want to build real authority. A tweet stating you are tired or just about to hit the sack is not what your audience is interested in.

Use Action Words

Just like the least engagement words, Zarrella also created a list of high-engagement words. Again, no prizes for guessing—the words that elicited maximum response are "help," "follow," "how to," and "retweet." If you implicitly ask your followers to perform an action, they are more likely to do it. These words emphasize more of the audience and what they are supposed to do rather than the tweet sender.

Tweet the Same Content Several Times

No, this doesn't make you a spammer like popular social media marketing perception would have you believe. There was a prevailing belief until recently that the social media audience is always looking for new content.

While that's partly true, practically, a lot of your followers will not be exposed to a brilliantly written blog if you only share it once.
The benefits of sharing content more than once are that you cover people from varied time zones, ensure greater exposure for your content, and reach out to new readers.

Re-posting content isn't as much a no-no as it's made out to be. Go ahead and repost popular blogs to attract new audience members and widen the reach of your content to build authority.

Keep it Between One to Four Tweets Each Day

Tweeting multiple times can make your audience immune to your tweets, especially if they are more marketing or sales focused. Like everything in excess, they will stop paying attention to what you have to say if you barrage their feed by tweeting throughout the day.

You don't want to come on too aggressively with your marketing strategy and annoy followers.

While responding to tweets or direct messages is perfectly acceptable, keep your tweets limited to about one to four tweets a day.

Chapter 4

Building Authority with Instagram

Building a social media brand is all about connecting with your audience and engaging them. It is about sharing, interacting with, and endorsing content. You need to hit a stride while interacting with your audience to show your brand some love.

Imagine how much more powerful the process of sharing and interacting would be if it is done through an image sharing site. Here are some top tips for Instagrammers to engage their audience and build authority.

Look for Influencers

Pairing your brand's voice with a popular voice within the industry is a great way to widen your reach and gain more authority among followers. Who are the star Instagrammers you want to network with to spread your brand name and share stories?

Start with entry level influencers, who have about 6k to 25k followers. These fellow Instagrammers are also looking to shine big on the platform by building their image portfolio; they will most likely be happy to share the images of your products they fancy.

Tier 2 influencers will be those featuring a following between 25k to 100k followers. Since these influencers have a far wider reach, they may charge you to promote your products and services or ask for products in exchange for recommendations.

A lot of Instagrammers who are mothers are known to recommend childcare products and/or services in exchange for products or payment.

If you have a marketing budget, engaging the services of an "InstaCeleb" may help you reach your target audience.

An important to thing to keep in mind if you take this authority-building route is to ensure that influencers are promoting your brand more organically and less aggressively. Followers can easily tell when a post is being promoted out of sheer passion and when it is a paid promotion.

You can proactively send out samples of your products to these influencers. Take time out to research their preferences if you want your product to resonate with them.

Look through their profiles and investigate their Instagram personalities. What's the overall vibe of their account? Why do you think they'd be good ambassadors for your brand? Ensure that you send samples that you feel are a good fit for their persona.

Leverage the power of influencers who have a huge following by reaching out to these experts and partnering with them for mutual gain. One of the best ways to gain exposure to their audience is to do expert round-ups.

For instance, if you run a cooking blog or cookery related business, you can invite top influencers in your industry to be featured in an expert round-up where all the experts share their favorite recipes. Afterward, you can be assured these folks will post a link of the round-up where they feature on their feed.

Can you imagine your reach when each of these experts with their own thousands of followers share a link to your blog or site?

Come up with a nice image to go with the round-up and ensure that you approach these experts professionally by stating why you admire their work and why you'd like to have them featured along with other industry experts. This strategy can work well on almost every social media network.

Find the Right Photos and Photographers

It doesn't end with finding potential influencers. You need to have a bank of high quality, creative, and evocative images that you'd like to share with your followers. You can find them on Instagram or other outsourcing sites.

Keep in mind that the quality of your product and service images demonstrates the quality of your products and services to potential customers. High quality pictures are non-negotiable on Instagram.

Also, keep in mind that Instagram is a platform for sharing creative visual stories and coming up with different ways to share regular images. It isn't simply about clicking pictures of your products and uploading them to impress users. Instagram is more of a lifestyle medium.

You need to be resourceful when it comes to posting on Instagram. Share everything from behind-the-scenes images of your workplace to pictures about your latest office luncheon to presenting your products innovatively.

For instance, if you retail funky fashion jewelry, you can get your dog to model for a neckpiece or your cat to sport a ring on its paws. Anything that promotes your products in novel, creative, and attention-grabbing ways is welcome.

Have a Clear Brand Personality

You need to figure out how you want to come across to your customers on a business Instagram account. You can share images randomly on your personal account; however, brands are different. They must have a clear, consistent and unique persona that echoes with the audience.

Do you want to come across as a witty, fun, and approachable brand? Or a more pensive and serious business? Are you focusing more on selling your products and services through the platform or do you simply want to get people talking about your brand?

When the brand persona and social media marketing objective is thoroughly worked, your task becomes easier. Use a mix of actionable techniques combined with personal narratives. Instagram followers love a hint of personal touch.

You can have a combination of advice, personal narratives, reflections, motivational quotes, and actionable problem-solving tips backed by high quality images. Once you gauge audience response, you can continue the themes and/or content sharing styles that resonate with your audience. Tie what works into your promotion plan seamlessly.

One sneaky tip on finding out what your customers love is to simply hop over to a popular competitor's account to discover what they are sharing. You can also scour most-visited blogs or sites in your niche to see what they are doing to win rave audience reviews.

Make Your Images More Searchable with Hashtags

Hashtags are not just for teenage pop icons and lifestyle-flaunting celebrities. They can be powerfully used to increase awareness about your brand's current activities and help viewers locate topics and images that truly interest them.

Start by drafting a post, followed by including your hashtags in the comments section. Attaching appropriate, memorable, and relevant hashtags makes it easier for users who are not following you to find your pictures. Instagram allows a maximum of 30 hashtags for each post.

A little-known yet powerful way to assign hashtags to your images is by compiling a list of your industry or niche's most frequently used hashtags.

Create the list in the notes section of your smartphone and simply copy and paste it in the comments section after creating a post. The best part is, it will not appear spammy since the comment will be hidden once your post gathers at least 5 comments. Neat trick? You bet.

Use a Powerful Call to Action

While plenty of businesses are using Instagram to promote their products or services, they are not capitalizing on its virtues because they fail to inform people where to go after browsing their images.

You can incorporate a strong call to action just about anywhere - right from your profile bio section to selected posts. A fun and attention-grabbing call to action works optimally for Instagram, since you only have about 150 characters to play with.
You can direct your customers to a landing page where they can sign up for some freebies, or you can send them to your home page. If you are posting images of your products or services, use the comments section to direct them to pages where they can complete the sale if they are interested.

Utilize Regramming

User-generated content is one of the best ways to keep you on top of the audience engagement game. Regramming is a term assigned to the practice of posting photos from other Instagram accounts to your feed with proper permission and credit from the owner of the image (accounts of your followers).

The advantage of this is that the photo creator gets an endorsement as well as exposure for the image in the form of a share. Your fans will feel thrilled that you care enough for them to support their content, which will turn casual followers into loyalists.

The benefit of this strategy is that your feed is filled with lots of high quality, user-generated content, thus saving you valuable time you might have spent creating even more of your own images. This isn't about being lazy; it's about a mutually beneficial strategy for you and your followers.

Maintain a healthy mix of original and user-generated content. You don't want to lose your identity by constantly posting images created by others. Recommended images will encourage your fans to post even more images, thus creating a productive cycle of user-generated pictures that you can use for boosting engagement.

Some of the ways to encourage users to share more pictures is by creating a powerful hashtag that inspires them to contribute. You can also organize a weekly or monthly photo contest and give away prizes to the most highly voted images.

Create Discussion Prompting Captions

Your Instagram caption should not be an afterthought. It's a given that Instagram is a visual social network; this is exactly why you should use its limited characters optimally for highest impact.

Think of your caption as a solid value addition for boosting engagement. Some of the planet's most popular Instagrammers are always telling stories, raising questions, using interesting hashtags, or incorporating emoji cleverly in their captions.

Spend some time crafting a compelling caption that stimulates conversation. Don't just use it to describe the image or tell users what they can already see. Instead, use it as an extension of your image. Bring the picture to life by creating an aura of popularity around it. Come up with copy that your audience can identify with or that triggers a raw emotion in them.

Make sure that the caption is consistent with the overall tone and vibe of your brand. Come up with creative prompts that will allow your audience to add to your storytelling or conversation.

Think of something creative such as "I'd rather be at..." or "there's never a wrong time for..." Leave captions open for them to come up with their own clever versions. Find a unique, identifiable, and personal brand voice, and come up with interesting captions that are completely in sync with this voice.

Steal Competitors' Followers

These are a bunch of people already interested in your products and services. The best way to draw your closest competitor's followers is by following them, liking an image, or commenting on one of their photos.

If you are running a local business, adding your location will help you create some familiarity for potential followers.

Start by following about 100 followers of your competitors. Next, follow another 100 followers but like one image posted by each of them. Lastly, follow another 100 followers and comment on at least one image posted by each of those 100 users.

Check your "follow back" statistics and keep repeating with different competitors and their followers. Ensure the followers you are targeting are not just part of a general audience but are people who are really interested in your products and services.

Chapter 5

LinkedIn—the Ultimate Authority-Building Channel

Have you ever witnessed a flash mob? We simply stop everything we are doing to watch them, but what happens when the novelty of the situation wears off in a few minutes? We leave and get back to our earlier activity. Do you know who organized the performance or directed it? Most likely not. Is the experience short-lived? You bet. We forget about it faster than we can say "flash mob." Now, imagine witnessing an opera at a fancy venue.

Don't you watch with rapt attention, completely enamored by the well-orchestrated performance for the gifted artists? You applaud and appreciate them, and you know you'll be coming back.

Think about positioning yourself as an opera performer who invests in long terms gains rather than a flash mob participant who attracts more knee-jerk and short-lived attention.

Find and Share Fantastic Content from Influencers

To find top influencer content on LinkedIn, all you need to do is go to the Interests option and select the Influencers dropdown. Now, filter the posts based on the week's top posts or the latest posts or today's most popular posts, etc.

If you want to share influencer content on your network daily, just select the Top Posts Today option, so that you are well on your way to sharing the most popular topical posts within your network.

Find the best posts and schedule them to be posted on your feed through the day. The early bird gets the worm? Oh, yes. On social media, it always helps to be one of the first ones to let the information out.

It demonstrates to your followers that you are privy to insider information which owes to your strong network of connections. Therefore, the quicker the content is posted on your feed, the more likely users are to view you as an industry authority.

If they've already read the piece on several other feeds, your shared content loses its appeal. Ensure that you follow people you find truly inspirational. These experts will show up in your customized news section.

Ensure that the content you share is thought provoking, well-written, and doesn't state the obvious. Choose posts that will add value to people's business or professional lives and gives them something new to chew on.

Go to the All Influencers sections and find some of the best industry influencers to follow. You will find a drop down that allows you to find influencers by applying filters, such as "most followed experts."

While you should definitely follow top influencers from your industry, do not restrict it only to them. Open up your network by connecting with other inspiring and experienced professionals, from whom you can learn a thing about business strategies and organization management.

Go for thought leaders who are known for coming up with original, off-beat, and interesting ideas. Sharing their valuable and trail-blazing content also helps you establish yourself as a top content curator among your connections.

Build Connections by Being a Groupie

LinkedIn's groups are one of the best ways to break the ice with experts and build solid professional networks. Select the groups that you want to be a part of wisely, as LinkedIn only allows you to join a maximum of 50 groups.

Choose the most active and popular groups. A good tip to get noticed quickly is by joining local groups. You will have the advantage of becoming the big fish and enjoying better leverage than the larger groups.

Avoid becoming a part of groups that aren't beneficial or have a low level of activity. To exit a group, go to the particular group page, select More (from the navigation bar), followed by Your Settings, and finally click on Leave Group to exit.

There will always be handful of members who contribute to the discussions in a meaningful and engaging manner with well-thought responses. View them as your prospective partners. Reach out to them via LinkedIn's InMails feature that allows two members belonging to the same group have a one-on-one conversation.

Connect with group members on a regular basis to discover different collaborative opportunities. Start by offering a little background information about yourself and your company's products and services. Tell them why you appreciate their valuable contributions and how you can help their business.

If you enjoyed reading a specific piece of content they created or shared, or a comment they added within the group discussion, mention it to let them know you keenly follow their stuff.

Use the LinkedIn Publishing Platform

One of the most fantastic ways to gain leverage for your ideas on LinkedIn is by creating top notch content on its publishing platform. Crafting useful, insightful, analytic, and industry-relevant content puts you in the fast lane of the authority-building highway.

Try and figure out what information and solutions people are after from your group discussions with industry folks. Then draft your own well-researched and original post about it, which can also be shared within the group.

Creating useful and information-rich content consistently positions you as an industry insider. It also reflects your capability to come up with original thoughts and a keenness to help people.

Don't simply rehash or rewrite content you find on other sources. Try to make complicated concepts sound simple with stories and analogies. Provide your own unusual interpretation or angle to a widely discussed topical issue.

People appreciate original and different angles when it comes to creating content on a subject that's already done to death on social media.

Use a variety of media formats to grab your audience's attention and keep them glued to your content. Infographics, images, videos, charts, and so on can add a whiff of freshness to your articles. Avoid being banal and focus on getting your facts and figures right. Few things can shake your credibility like a smart reader pointing out discrepancies in your content.

To boost the sharing of your posts, address specific issues or problems in your content. For instance, if you run a recruitment company, you can offer your expert strategies for reducing high attrition rates and retaining employees. Include high quality images to go with the post to add more meat to it (all right, more greens if you are a vegetarian or vegan).

Stick to posting about a couple of status updates daily, along with a weekly published blog post. Play with LinkedIn Pulse. It is one of the platform's coolest tools, which sends your customers weekly email alerts about your posts. This helps you stay on top of their awareness and keeps them more engaged.

Keep in mind that your last three published articles show up in your profile right below the profile photograph. This offers greater visibility to your content.

Anyone exploring your profile can click on See More to view the content, which is why the content is so important for creating a stellar first impression. Also, each time you publish a post on LinkedIn Publisher, a notification is received by all your connections.

A super way to draw the attention of your connections to posts that may be interesting to them is to simply tag them (@followed by their name).

This ensures that even if they haven't been active on the network, they receive a mail linking to the post where they are tagged. This makes your content more accessible and visible to connections who are truly interested in it.

Endorse Others' Posts and Content

Yes, you can post all the valuable and insightful content, but keep in mind that your connections have hundreds and thousands of other connections, all creating fantastic content.

How then do you stay on top of the game? How do you draw attention to yourself in the midst of all the noise? Simple. Spare some time every day to browse through your feed and comment on the really good stuff. You can also like and share the content ahead as an endorsement of its ingenuity.

If you consistently like and share the content of many connections, they'll appreciate your endorsement and get familiar with you. They will most likely check out the stuff you are posting and will return the favor by liking and sharing your content too, thus creating a powerful content endorsing synergy.

Target different connections over a period of time, and in a couple of months, you may boast of a highly engaged network of connections.

Social media is about establishing fruitful give-and-take relationships. Maintain a healthy balance of creating your own content as well as endorsing content created by others.

Endorsing other content will help you raise engagement, while crafting fabulous content will keep your connections interested.

Profile Views

LinkedIn offers you pretty comprehensive statistics about your profile views so you know exactly who is viewing your profile and how it can be optimized for your target audience. You can view the name, location, industry, and other similar details of users visiting your profile. That's not all, though; it also shows you exactly how these people came across your profile, along with a graph that reveals the tally of views you've garnered to date, and profile viewing trends over the last 90 days.

These insights act as useful clues for determining who your target audience is and what needs to be highlighted in your profile to create a favorable impression.

Create the Perfect Profile Headline

People on social media, especially on a business platform such as LinkedIn, do not have much time to read through elaborate descriptions and introductions. They often judge the merit of a profile via a snappy and cleverly crafted headline that sums up your brand or business persona.

Though describing yourself in a few words may seem like an impossible proposition (you are a unique and complex personality like everyone else with experiences, preferences, strengths, and goals), you have to make an effort to distill your headline to a few impactful words.

Your current job title is your default headline. If you do not create a separate headline, LinkedIn automatically displays your present job title, which can be a tad uninspiring.

Creating a customized headline summing up your profile and offering a solid value proposition can pay off big time, so it is totally worth the trouble.

To customize your headline for your audience, use terms that will be recognized by your target audience without much effort.

Don't try to mislead your audience by creating fancy and non-straightforward terms. For instance, if you are a sales representative, don't try to masquerade under Account Development Manager or other ambiguous terms.

Make it easy for target users to identify your profile and industry. Do not include role-specific or industry related jargon that your target audience will have trouble understanding. Keep the lingo compelling, straightforward, and professional, without making it too technical.

Do not simply stop at describing yourself. Add a powerful value proposition for the user too. Let them know what is in it for them. Your customers need to understand how you can contribute to their lives with your products or services. You can go with something like a job title followed by a value addition.

For example, you could write Make-up Artist: Helping Brides Make Their Big Day Even More Special with Incredible Bridal Make-up. In this way, you've established that you are a professional make-up artist at the beginning on the headline, so your audience knows exactly who you are. This is followed by offering an implicit value proposition to the target audience – brides.

Another example could be Kitchen Appliance Specialist: Saving households time and effort with faster cooking solutions. There is a clear, definite and attention-grabbing value that instantly resonates with your audience. You can also include your brand's value proposition or tagline if you have a well-crafted tagline that more or less sums up the benefit you offer. Try scouring your customer testimonials if you are having trouble coming up with a value proposition.

Few things put people off like someone patting themselves on the back on a professional social network. Your audience is not looking for self-complimenting individuals who can't seem to see beyond themselves.

Avoid using over-the-top adjectives such as top performing, best, expert, superior, winning, etc. These fancy titles hold more credibility when they originate from your customers and not when you blow your own horn in a bid to attract users. Adjectives such as these will make you come across as more arrogant and less approachable, which is definitely not the impression you want to create.

Flaunt your skills by including positive customer experience stories and customer feedback in your profile's summary section. You will draw high quality and good conversion rates if you get the nuances of a crafting a killer headline right.

Create Fantastic Business and Showcase Pages

Create a well-written and compelling company page to establish a strong LinkedIn presence. Include a high-resolution profile image and cover photo. You can get it designed by a professional graphic designer on one of the freelance job networks. Write a snappy, effective, and interesting company description of no more than 2,000 characters.

Use the company specialty section to include relevant industry keywords to make your profile more accessible through search engines. You should also offer details about your organization including industry type, size, contact options, and other vital information. Ensure all details are properly filled in to make it easier for potential customers to understand your company and contact you.

How do you create a company page? Just navigate to the Interests option and select the Companies option from a drop-down menu. The page's right hand corner will display a Create a Company Page option. Click on the Create button to begin creating your company page.

Showcase pages act as an extension of your company page. Think of them as other pages on your website, with the company page being the home page or About Us page. You may want to create other pages to highlight new products or services, promote upcoming events, or cross-market other brands.

Though these pages are linked to your primary company page, they are standalone entities, which can be used to promote different aspects of your business.

Each of them can have their own group of followers, feature individual content, and boast of exclusive functions. To build your showcase page, simply go to the company profile section. Navigate to the Edit drop down option and click on the yellow Create a Showcase Page button. Now follow the instructions to build showcase pages of your choice.

Showcase pages are more intensive than general company pages in the sense that they include more detailed information about a single aspect of your company. For instance, say your company is hosting an event. Now, you can't include complete details about the event on your company page. You may just offer a snapshot of the event of the main page, while your event showcase page can have more detailed information for those who are only interested in the event.

These pages help you categorize information about multiple aspects of your business. You can also boost the visual element of each category by adding relevant cover photos to your showcase pages, like a specially created event banner for the above example.

Avoid using your brand or company name as a showcase page title. It doesn't reveal much about what the page is dedicated to. Rather, select a descriptive name which summarizes what the page stands for and sets the right content expectations for your audience.

Include important, industry-related keywords while titling the page so it can be found easily through LinkedIn's search feature.

Make Your Profile Visually Rich

It beats me why so many LinkedIn users fail to capitalize on its Professional Portfolio function for boosting their authority. You can do everything from adding photos to videos to image-rich articles to SlideShare presentations. Use this feature to build your credibility and authority by including screenshots or infographics.

Other things you can add using this feature include your speaker videos, product launch event videos, special corporate programs or projects, press coverage received by your company, work portfolio (comprising some of the best work you've completed for past clients), and screenshots for building social proof (think tweets where your company or brand has been flatteringly mentioned).

Give your LinkedIn profile the ultimate makeover, and you'll be amazed by the results you'll achieve by making these simple yet high-impact changes. Visual content offers a less time-consuming and more valid proof of your expertise.

For instance, your profile description may include something about your company being covered by the press, but your prospective customers may not even bother to read to that point, and it may not hold much weight. However, if you include screenshots of your press coverage, they will not only boost your credibility but also make it easier for users to quickly scan through your profile for getting an idea about the strength of your company and products or services.

Just because LinkedIn is a professional network doesn't mean it has to be an uninspiring virtual version of your resume. Pack some punch into it by using cutting-edge social media features to increase your exposure and build authority.

Chapter 6

Pinterest for Building Authority

Let's share an interesting fact that you most likely did not know about Pinterest. Did you know that different categories of pins are popular on different days of the week on Pinterest? While fitness is popular on Monday, quotes peak in popularity on Wednesday (maybe this has to do with the mid-week crisis).

Similarly, humor is extremely popular on Friday (there my theory gains momentum) and travel-related pins work wonderfully well on a Saturday. Think this is interesting? Well, it's just the beginning. Pinterest offers you a visually stunning and interesting platform to gain exposure for your products or services or content. Read on to find out how you can use it to boost your exposure and build authority.

Create a Pinterest Account

Rather than using your blog or company name while creating a Pinterest account, add a more personal name and image. Keep in mind Pinterest is all about user-generated images and as such, having an interesting and unique personal name will pique your audience's curiosity over a boring sounding company name (I know we are still suffering from the LinkedIn hangover).

Stick to a name that resonates with women, since the network currently features about 80% female users. Not that you can't use a masculine name, but try to keep it more real, personal, and friendly.

The reason I mention creating a personal account over a business account is that users on Pinterest don't take too kindly to self-promotion. It is seen more as a platform for sharing interesting ideas and creative solutions than blatant marketing.

If you're solely focused on marketing your website or products, you are better off on another social media platform like Twitter, LinkedIn, or even Facebook. If you don't fancy a personal account, try creating theme-based accounts instead of business accounts.

For instance, if you run a travel agency focusing on several destinations, instead of creating a business account, try to create different accounts for different travel themes such as romantic holidays and honeymoon, destination weddings, adventure tourism, eco and wildlife tourism, etc.

Once you create the profile or profiles, write appropriate descriptions to give an idea about what exactly you plan to pin. Keep your introduction friendly and personal.

Avoid business or marketing lingo on Pinterest, as it doesn't feature an innately corporate vibe. The profile description can mention some value addition or benefit offered by you (using the right keywords) without overtly promoting it. This makes it easy for users to locate your pins using the network's search feature.

Keep in mind that users will make split-second decisions on whether to follow you based on the first impression you create with your profile. Make it nothing short of stunning. Include a happy image of yourself or a picture that aptly describes what your profile is all about. Leaving the profile picture section empty makes you come across as a fake and spammy account.

Create Pinboards

Once you are all set with the account, go ahead and create a pinboard. Think of a title that would resonate with your target users. Creating too many pinboards can dilute their impact, especially if you are using the network for business. Pinterest users are more interested in following stand-alone pinboards than an entire account. Focus on a single, coherent theme for each board. Do not have more than 5 pinboards, as you will find it challenging to manage them.

Here's a short guide on creating pinboards that actually work.

Tap or click on the "create a board" icon on your profile page. Include a write-up with specific keywords for every board. Ensure that you pick the right category for the pin board such as travel, fitness, food, etc. This is crucial if you want to be found by the right audience.

Once this is done, go to the Pinterest search to the top left corner of your screen and start a search. The search should be filtered to Boards and not Pins. Find a few boards that feature similar themes as yours.

When you come across a few boards, start following them and pin a few of their interesting images on your freshly created pinboard. You can pin any piece of content by clicking on the red pin icon that appears on the left corner of every image.

Follow and pin images from around 10-15 different boards (from different accounts) with the same theme. When you have about 20 pins for the first board, create your other boards in a similar fashion.

It's always a good practice to follow pin boards you pin from because the board creators are immediately sent a notification that you are following them, which most likely results in them following you back. This is how you build your initial followers.

Leverage the Power of Group Boards

Pinterest group boards are just like other social media groups. They are community boards created by users to invite other people for pinning. Some Pinterest boards have thousands of group members and followers.

Now, if you are a member of a Pinterest group board, each time you or someone from the group pins on the board, the pin is displayed on the top page feed of each person following the board. The larger group boards are more likely to show up in Google search results, awarding you more clout.

Create Your Own Group Board

Your group boards may not attract a large bunch of groupies, but it is always a great tip to convert personal pinboards into group boards for boosting authority once you have acquired a few dozen followers. All you have to do is go to the board, click on Edit Board (look at the center of the board).

Make the necessary changes using the Who Can Pin section. Keep in mind that you can only invite users who are both following you and being followed by you. Choose the ones you want to add. A notification or email will be sent to them informing them about the group add.

When users accept the invite, the group board displays on their account page, and can be followed by anyone who comes across it. This gives more exposure to your board, and helps you garner greater Pinterest authority. Even with just 50 group members, there are 50 spots where users can find you to follow you.

You would do well to invite the larger influencer pinners to your group board, though they may not show much interest in joining smaller groups.

Once you have a sizeable following, it will be much easier to build on it. However, in the initial stages you'd just have to contend with inviting your family and friends and following boards you like with the hope that they'll return the favor.

When you have a couple of hundred followers, scaling up to a thousand won't be as hard as building the initial 100-200 followers. Hence, do not give up in the initial stages. Stick on and keep pinning unique, original and relevant stuff that your target audience loves.

People on social media or any internet marketing medium seldom realize building the first few followers often takes maximum effort because that's when you are just establishing yourself and no one takes you seriously.

However, patience, persistence, and regular efforts at this stage often pay off hugely in the end when you are able to grow the following into thousands and even millions in the long run. All social media stars started with a handful followers and grew from there, taking one step at a time.

Get the Pinning Right

A majority of Pinterest users simply re-pin images from other boards on their Pinterest boards, thus creating a link back to another web page. If you plan to pin from your blog or website, ensure that the overall quality of the image is extremely high. Another thing to keep in mind is that you use only those pictures that you have legal permission to use.

Do not simply scrape images off a simple Google image search. You can use stock image services or find images on Wikimedia Commons or Flickr Creative Commons. Ensure that you read and comply with the terms of use of each image very carefully. Here are some quick expert tips on creating the perfect pins

1. Vertical images are more effective than horizontal ones on Pinterest.

2. Human faces may work wonderfully on Instagram; however, on Pinterest they result in very few repins.

3. Images that include a clear call to action enjoy a click-through rate that is 80% more than those without a well-defined call to action. If you are using social media for marketing and promotion, you need to tell your audience what to do if they are interested in your products or services. Don't just tease them and leave them hanging.

4. Some of the most popular pins on Pinterest are the "how-to" guides and tutorials. Pinterest users love DIY stuff so any useful and relevant step-by-step tutorial can get you plenty of repins from an interested audience. Tutorials enjoy about 42% of repins. Infographics work very well on the Pinterest platform.

5. Warm, bright, and eye-caching colors work much better on Pinterest compared to cool shades. Go ahead and use the reds and oranges generously.

It is recommended that you spread your pinning activities throughout the day instead of binge-pinning for half an hour. Pin about 4-5 times a day, adding a single pin each time on the group board. Avoid filling group boards with the same blog and website pins; it can lead to a ban. Short and valuable pinning sessions are much better for increasing your credibility quotient.

If you are interested in posting pins from your URL, just create a personal pinboard alongside your primary boards that you plan to convert into group boards eventually. This way you will have greater flexibility than group boards to add your personal URL pins to the board.

Title them correctly so users know exactly what they can look forward to. For instance, Beach Travel Articles or Best Diet Recipes or Effective Fitness Tips, etc. These boards can be used for pinning content that you want to frequently share with users.

Keep in mind that the largest chunk of Pinterest users comprises of American women. Hence, for maximizing results, you need to keep in mind USA time zones.

The most optimal times for pinning include post-lunch, late afternoons, and late evenings. If you are going to pin from another country, work out the USA time zones correctly to pin at the best possible time.

Just to ensure more variety, try to include pins from various websites and not just a single source. Well, you aren't expected to have half a dozen sites in the beginning, so it's a neat trick to alternate between posting from your own URL and other URLs.

Keep your personal pinboard as the primary source board and begin pinning from there all the way down to your other group Pinterest boards. These can be both groups created by you and groups you have joined.

Use each board to add a mixture of images from various URLs. This way you don't come across a spammer who is simply here to self-promote. When people see how you add interesting and valuable content from other sites and that you aren't just focused on peddling your products and services, they will be more likely to check out your website or blog.

Conclusion

Thank you for downloading *Social Media Marketing: Strategies to Capture and Engage Your Audience While Quickly Building Authority*.

I sincerely hope this book helped you understand little-known expert strategies that can be used to engage your audience and build authority across multiple social media platforms. The objective was to offer you a handy guide that is easy to understand and can get you started with your social media marketing immediately, with great results.

The book is packed with loads of simple yet actionable and effective tips that can boost your audience engagement and brand authority within a short span of time. I hope the nuggets of wisdom shared in the book inspire you to create some of your own strategies in line with what works best for your brand.

The next obvious step is to take action now that you have a powerhouse of information. Knowledge without action is a complete waste. Start by creating a well-planned social media marketing strategy by incorporating the techniques you learned here.

Research thoroughly. Know where your target users hang out, what appeals to them, what drives them, and other similar factors to create content that will enthrall them and keep them coming back for more.

Building authority on social media is a relentless process. You have to keep at it until you see something working and then just scale it up from there. But you need to start. Start immediately. Today. Now.

Social Media Marketing

Tips + Tricks to Build Credibility

Chapter 1

Social Media Marketing – An Introduction

How does one do "real world" business? If we want our early morning coffee, we simply scuttle into a Starbucks, grab our coffee, and rush off. Similarly, if we want to fill our car with gas, we land up at the gas station, get the gas, and drive away. The focus is on getting done with the business first and moving ahead. Getting the service takes precedence over forming relationships or connecting with people.

Using social media is the antithesis of this. The social media marketplace doesn't just place building meaningful relationships over selling, but actually makes it the bedrock of running a successful business. Everything revolves around the principles of building successful relationships. When used successfully, social media offers customers value before selling to them, and focuses on forging a strong brand identity.

According to a 2016 survey, 78 percent of Americans have a social media profile. The global social media user base figure is a staggering 1.96 million and is slated to expand to about 205 billion in 2018. This opens up a whole new world for entrepreneurs to do business by connecting with people and forming meaningful relationships with people from all over the world.

Imagine if you were to ignore the power of social media because you do not understand or it seems too complicated. Any idea how much money you would be leaving on the table for competitors to swallow?

Social media gives you tons of opportunities to build your authority and credibility in a topic or industry. It gives you myriad tools, features, applications and functions through which you can "wow" your audience. It adds panache to your marketing and promotional campaigns. Social media offers you the opportunity to share your expertise with a large audience within seconds. It helps spread the word about your products and services in a compelling manner.

Honestly, people are tired of being through the grind of traditional marketing methods. They've become highly immune to messages that blatantly "sell." Any messages related to sales and marketing ups their antennae, and compels them to run miles away.

As a customer, wouldn't you abhor a brand or person that simply tries to sell to you without connecting with your needs and desires? Wouldn't you rather have someone who helps you buy than someone who sells to you? Don't you love buying from people and companies that keenly tune in to your requirements and treat you as a unique human being as opposed to just another sales figure?

According to Social Media Examiner, about 86% of marketers declared that social media is vital for their ventures, with 49% picking Facebook as their main social media network. Think of social media as the business casual of the virtual world.

Yes, it's all serious business that's draped in nice, informal attire. It gives you the leeway to dress up in jeans and a chic loose tie (yes, okay, with pop-culture icons on it, too). However, you still conduct yourself in a professional and courteous manner. Yes, most social media networks encourage you to employ a friendly and breezy vibe, though the underlying tone still remains professional and businesslike.

In a nutshell, social media is your very own unique broadcasting channel that allows you to socialize with an audience, not unlike a television or radio channel that's constantly airing content. Everything that you put in this medium of mass communication in essence represents the values you stand for, your brand identity, and messages you are trying to convey to your target audience.

Your posts have an impact on your audience. They have their own social circles comprising of family, friends, and business associates or thousands of followers. The followers are influenced and inspired by them. Imagine the sheer effect of a powerfully communicated message on a few of your followers.

If only a handful of your followers decide to share the message with thousands of their followers and those followers in turn decide to share with it with their followers, can you even imagine the result?

Social networks are your medium of mass communication. Is your channel the local cable network, or HBO? That's something only you can decide, although we will give you lots of invaluable tips, insider advice, and lesser-known social media marketing secrets.

Being on social media is akin to attending a party. You need to showcase yourself in the best possible manner for becoming popular, making a whole new bunch of friends, and even hunting for that special someone.

When you enter a party, you simply walk in, make yourself a drink, and start interacting with other folks. You may instantly lay your eyes on a potentially hot date or walk up to someone you are already familiar with.

Do you ever just walk up to these people and start selling to them by pontificating about your products or services? Do you tell them your latest stock of cleaning devices is available at amazingly discounted prices? People will mostly likely walk away in exasperation, thinking about how obnoxious you sound. Haven't we all met such a person at a party? A person who goes on endlessly about themselves without bothering to know if anyone is interested in listening—do they have enough people listening to them or taking them seriously? You can bet your last dime – no.

This is exactly how it works in the social media sphere. If you inform people about something they find fascinating (or may want to share with their loved ones) by being polite, considerate, respectful, funny, informative, and entertaining, they will sit up and take notice.

People like to engage in conversations that aren't just about the person conducting the conversation. They like to be a part of interactions based on shared interests and passions. They want to be heard in a meaningful and interactive conversation, rather than subjected to tiresome monologues.

There are no particular rules for how a person should conduct himself at a party or café, are there? Yet common sense directs us to behave and connect with potential friends in a specific manner. Social media is exactly like this. There really are no rigid rules, but common sense dictates the way we conduct our interactions.

Your social media community can be described as a garden. It won't flourish if you simply plant seeds and don't nurture it. A thriving garden can never be a short-term task. It is a life-long pursuit of seeding, feeding and watering, weeding, and harvesting. If one crop doesn't work for you despite your best efforts and a change in strategy, you move on to another crop (or another social media network).

Social media marketing is a brilliant combination of logic and emotions when it comes to capturing the attention of your audience. You can use a variety of videos, texts, images, infographics, and more to elicit favorable responses from your audience based on powerful emotions and sound logic.

You really have to move people to get them to take action if you want to improve your sales conversion figures (the number of prospective customers turning into actual buyers). If you want to convert aimlessly surfing prospective customers into loyal buyers, you have to offer them real value before selling to them.

You have to be able to win their trust. They have to see you or your brand as likeable, credible, trustworthy, and authoritative. Potential customers need to know you care about their requirements by consistently offering them more value.

If you are able to correctly pin down their needs, engage them in meaningful conversations, add value to their lives, and maintain a great relationship throughout – they will most likely be sold. Sometimes even the cleverest marketing professionals do not realize the importance of giving precedence to helping people buy over simply selling to them.

Social media is all about creating a meaningful buzz. Let's say you are putting up a table at a packed exhibition. You set up your stall, keep all the brochures and hand-outs ready for people to see, and wait for potential customers to come.

However, no one seems really interested in what you have to sell. A few people pass by, pick up some brochures, leaf through them, and leave. What's going wrong with your strategy here? You have everything in place – all the brochures, demonstration equipment, and fancy data sheets. Yet no one is lingering.

You notice that other tables are abuzz with interesting activities. There's a lot happening in terms of photo booths, conjuring artists, graffiti boards, presentations, fun demonstrations or giveaways. You give up because you realize you can't compete with the buzz, without realizing the actual principles that create the frenzy.

This is what social media is all about—engaging your audience by understanding what drives them. It is all about promoting yourself by holding forth interesting interactions rather than waiting to pounce on customers with your products or services, hoping they'll buy what you sell.

Marketers somehow live in a mythical bubble world where they believe people are just dying to buy whatever they are selling. It can't be any less true. People buy when you give them strong reasons to buy from you. And it is not as much about your product or service as it is about your brand or you.

People buy from other people or entities they can relate to. They need to identify with your brand values and feel a strong sense of belonging with what you are offering before becoming loyalists. In short, they need to buy your vision before they buy your products and services.

Social media platforms are brilliant for creating that vision and identity. People need to feel one with the products and services they are associating with. They want to align with products and services that are in tandem not just with their requirements but also with their fundamental values.

Think of social media as a large digital café—a café that runs on a national or international scale. You have all sorts of people walking in and out. Some are smart, empathetic, and courteous. Others are abusive and seem to enjoy garnering attention through inappropriate means. How you attract attention in the giant, international social media café is up to you.

Ever gone fishing? Did you learn it overnight? Chances are, not really, unless you were born in a pond. It took time, lots of effort, and a strong willingness to learn, right? You may have been disappointed with no bites, initially. Then you went ahead and fine-tuned your fishing skills by adopting different trial and error strategies.

You may have gradually realized exactly how to generate plenty of bites by understanding how specific species respond to your baiting techniques.

This is how you master social media, too. Nobody can master it in a day. It will be a dynamic and evolving learning process of trying to understand exactly what drives your customers. It will be about forging strong customer relationships by engaging them and offering them value.

It will be about creating a powerful identity, credibility, and authority for your brand. It is about identifying the "hot buttons" in your fish or target audience, and using those hot buttons to develop meaningful discussions that eventually lead to higher conversions. Simple? Yes. Easy? No. Possible? Very much so.

Thousands of small, mid-sized, and large businesses have leveraged the power of social media to create a stir about their products and services (and they certainly didn't master it overnight!). There's absolutely no reason for your brand to be left behind.

Think of traditional advertising techniques as fireworks compared to the bonfire of social media platforms. A grand fireworks display can be attention-grabbing, but it is also pricey, knee-jerk, monotonous, and short term.

In contrast, social media is like a solid and dependable bonfire. It takes more time to create, but is more affordable, long-term, and varied. The highly focused and engaging "bonfire" communities work relentlessly to keep the fire alive.

Think you don't know about social media well enough to jump into it? Plenty of us move into different cities and countries all the time. What happens when we land up in an altogether different country? Culture shock. You don't immediately earn the trust, respect and acceptance of the local community without learning about their unique customs, etiquette, norms, and behaviors.

Social Media Do's and Don'ts

Do have a solid plan in place. Without a cohesive plan and marketing and brand building strategy, your social media efforts will collapse like a pack of cards. You need to weave social media seamlessly into your organic and content marketing strategy. Create realistic goals and know the pulse of your target consumers.

Do establish your presence on relevant platforms. Much as you'd like to be omnipresent on social media, some networks may be better suited for the nature of your business than others. For instance, local cake shops and florists may benefit more from the visual appeal of Pinterest or Instagram over the more formal LinkedIn. Similarly, a large accounting corporation may benefit more from Twitter and LinkedIn over Pinterest. Understand the functions and features of each network and identify the one that can be best used to create an enticing buzz about your products or services.

Do strike the right balance between a casual-friendly approach and professionalism. Like we discussed in an analogy above, social media is like dressing up in business casual. You can be more relaxed in your attire but you still have to be professional in your approach.

Even it's a more casual or informal approach, it's business at the end of the day. Irrespective of the network and your brand tone, keep your spelling and grammar flawless, use authentic sources, and reinforce your statements with facts.

Do stay focused on your social media campaigns. As discussed earlier, do not expect overnight miracles from your social media pages. Many marketers believe that if they simply create a page, put up impressive graphics, and write valuable content, users will swarm like bees to their pages.

They are massively disappointed when people do not bother to check their profiles or pages and end up wondering where they went wrong. Go back to the exhibition analogy discussed earlier. Despite having everything ready, why couldn't you draw an audience? You simply gave up instead of changing your strategy.

You weren't generating enough action to engage your audience. Social media thrives on regular updates and audience engagement. It should be integral to your brand's daily routine. Jumping from one network or group to another will certainly not help. You need to be committed to planning and sticking to a long-term social media marketing strategy if you truly want to exploit its virtues.

Do not (and this is a big do not) use social networks as hard-selling tools. Social media is not only about generating leads and sales. Rather, view it as a ladder designed to bridge the gap between you and your prospective customers. At best, it is about familiarizing them with your brand, which can help them make future buying decisions. Sales pitches do not go with the vibe of Facebook posts or Twitter feeds. The sooner you realize this, the faster you can build a loyal audience base.

Social media is all about sharing your unique brand persona with your target audience. It is to establish your credibility and authority as a brand by way of value addition. It is about creating something likeable and desirable that people would want to be associated with. Selling comes much later. Potential customers need to connect with your brand before they buy.

Do not expect instant returns. Whether you use free or paid social media promotional methods, keep in mind you won't witness stellar results overnight. As with any online marketing medium, reaping profitable dividends will take time, effort, knowledge, and skills.

You may have to engage your audience on an everyday basis or try different engagement strategies to identify the ones that work best for your audience. Rather than simply building a group of followers you can sell to once, you have to focus on nurturing a bunch of potential customers you can sell to over and over by building a loyal fan base.

It requires effort, consistency and a keen will to connect with people. Seeing your efforts transform to fruition may take time, but those that hang in there are more likely to be generously rewarded.

Do create interesting, valuable, and engaging content. Offering value to your audience is key. One of the best ways to give out this value is by creating authoritative, compelling and useful content. This not just gives something back to your customers for following you, but also establishes your brand authority and credibility.

Sharing timely, regular, detailed, and thought-provoking content makes you come across a genius. It positions you as an influencer within your industry circle and among potential customers. Once you win their trust by establishing your authority in a domain, people are more likely to follow your recommendations.

They are more likely to listen to you, respect your opinion, and buy from you when they know how solid your industry knowledge is. It is no secret that people like to buy from experts who know their stuff. By all means, flash and share your expertise on social media.

Do listen to your audience. Much as it is about flaunting your unique persona and knowledge, social media is also about listening. As discussed previously, social media is about conversations over sales pitches. Ensure that you are completely tuned in to the needs, desires, driving factors, fears, and aspirations of your target audience by holding meaningful conversations.

Start debates, trigger important discussions, and promptly answer queries your followers may have. Structure your content, promotion, and brand building strategies around your audience's needs.

Of late, audiences respond more favorably to share- and "likes"-based recommendations. Stay competitive by involving them in discussions and constantly evolving according to their changing needs.

Do track response-engagement results. Find out which social networking platforms work best with your products or services. Get your feet wet in popular social network advertising programs. Keep tracking results generated by user activities. The information gathered can be used to tweak and personalize future campaigns.

When you track results, you know exactly what is resonating with your audience and what's not working as expected. This gives you the opportunity to constantly tweak your campaigns for building more effective engagement and drawing traffic to your page. It also gives the opportunity to gauge exactly which network a major chunk of your traffic is coming from, to help you leverage the power of that network.

Do use social media for social responsibility and socially beneficial initiatives. A great way to build credibility and a favorable social reputation is to launch socially relevant initiatives that contribute to the greater good of society. This helps you come across as a responsible and ethical organization that has got its heart in place.

Build a powerful brand equity by letting customers know that your organization isn't just about making profits but also contributing to society at large. Social media networks are the best way to enlist support for your noble initiatives on a massive scale in an organic manner. Create socially relevant initiatives that resonate with your brand values and the overall vision of your business.

For instance, Marriott hotels ran a check-in social media campaign that asked guests to check in virtually to enable the hospitality firm to contribute $2 to charity each time a guest checked into one of their properties. The promotional campaign intended to harness the power of social media to create a buzz about the hotels by contributing to the greater good for humanity. The campaign not only brought them a large audience but also created a persona of a socially responsible organization that cares about humanity at large.

Chapter 2

Powerful Tips for Building Credibility on Facebook

The Set-Up

Start by getting your basics in place. Ensure you have a complete and fully optimized Facebook page. Load the pages with details about your business and awesome content. How do you expect people to like pages that don't even have a profile picture?

Take extra effort to optimize your page, add high-resolution images, and a few posts before unveiling the page to the public. Key elements needed for a completed profile are a profile photo, cover photo, detailed About Us section, contact number, and website URL.

Storytelling

Fans love when you bring in the human factor and tell stories around it. They like to know more about a brand through its behind-the-scenes stories, its people, and its history. Your brand becomes more human, personal, and likeable through the sharing of intimate stories.

Storytelling is one of the most powerful ways of communicating and connecting with people for their personal appeal. People can remember stories that strike a chord with them for a long time. They are more likely to connect with a brand once they know the brand's inside story.

By sharing the stories of your brand's origins, successes, failures, challenges, lessons, and more, you're taking audience relationships to entirely new levels.

You should examine the profile of WWE star Dwayne "The Rock" Johnson to see how he has mastered the art of connecting with his audience via the medium of stories.

Create Valuable and Interesting Content

Demonstrate your expertise and knowledge in a specific domain by creating and sharing engaging and valuable content. Nothing spells credibility killer more than a ghost Facebook page with negligible engagement in the form of likes, comments, and shares.

It is tough to establish your credibility when there are no interactions happening on your page. Create through-provoking and detailed blog posts. Build stunning infographics (use Canva and Picmonkey) that people won't think twice before sharing.

Share engaging, evocative, and entertaining images or videos from the web. Sharing extraordinary and attention-grabbing content is a foolproof way to gain brand credibility. Scoop.it and Postplanner are great content curation tools.

Build Social Proof

Building social proof is essential for building brand trust and credibility. Facebook allows you to leverage the power of social proof incredibly well.

When you have a huge circle of Facebook fans who consistently engage in liking, sharing, and commenting on your posts, you send out impressive social credibility signals. Potential customers realize how popular your brand is, and they are immediately drawn to it.

Let us go back to our party analogy. Aren't people always curious about the person surrounded by the most people in a party? Don't you feel tempted to check out why that person is drawing so much attention? It is much the same with social proof on Facebook.

Potential customers will always find high engagement pages attractive. Some of the best ways to build credibility are case studies, honors and recognitions, client testimonials, photographs with industry leaders, media coverage, and your published articles and books. Include images of trainings or conferences you attend or certifications you earn.

Customer testimonials are a great way to showcase how your products or services or content have benefitted people, which in turn builds tremendous brand credibility. Include an image of a happy customer (after seeking permission of course) and their account of how your product or service benefitted them.

Be Present and Consistent

A Facebook page is only as good or bad as the person or people maintaining it. One of the bedrocks of social media marketing is consistency. You have to keep updating your followers' newsfeeds with posts at regular intervals. It may be once a day, thrice a day, or once every two days.

Work out a frequency that works best in grabbing the attention of your audience without annoying them. Be consistent and keep posting at planned intervals. Once a day is a good rule of thumb for most businesses. Creating an editorial schedule and content calendar is a great way to give your fans an idea of what they can expect.

Here's a handy guide on scheduling posts.

Start by drafting your post as you usually do. Attach the required images, videos, tags, links etc. to other sources or simply leave it as a text-only post.

In the lower left hand corner of the post, click the clock symbol. You will now be able to choose the year, month, date, and time you want to publish the post.

At the time of this writing, you can only schedule posts up to 6 months in advance. Also, time can only be scheduled at 00, 10, 20, and so on. So, you won't be able to schedule a post for, say, 3:15. Language and geo targeting can also be added to the post. All you need to do is click on the globe icon (public) and make the required changes.

Once everything is done, click on the Schedule button (the one in blue). Make sure you come back to your posts to witness the activity once they have been posted.

Top Notch Customer Support

This is an absolute no-brainer. Provide high value and unmatched customer support to your Facebook fans. Show them you are real by acknowledging and addressing their concerns.

Few things can wreck your online reputation like an incensed customer who was dissatisfied with your products or services and failed to get a response from you. This would be a certain death sentence for brand credibility.

Ignoring customers shows you aren't bothered about them once you get their money, which definitely means you are not getting their money again. It is a widely known fact in marketing circles that acquiring new customers is way more expensive than retaining existing ones.

Here are some golden rules for offering high-class customer service on Facebook to boost your credibility.

Customers seek speedy resolution to their problems and queries on Facebook. Promptly acknowledging your customer's concerns and getting to work on resolving their issue as soon as possible will help you earn plenty of brownie points, and more business.

Customers take to addressing their queries on social media to make sure they are heard. When you acknowledge their query, you assure them that you are concerned about resolving their issue.

Like every customer service medium, customer service on Facebook is about catering to your customer's needs by going that extra mile. If the customer has faced an issue related to your products or services, rather than getting defensive and showing yourself in a poor light, accept responsibility for the blooper and apologize if needed. Sometimes, customers are not even looking for a resolution in the form of a replacement or refund; all they want from you is the acknowledgment that you goofed up. Even if you don't know when the issue will be resolved, respond with a holding post that reassures the customer that you are working on it.

Keep informing your customer about the resolution status. They will be more than happy to wait if you acknowledge their issue and keep them in the loop about the resolution's progress.

One of the most important objectives of a Facebook presence is to resolve product- or service-related issues as quickly as possible to ensure customers go back happy after the interaction.

A customer complaint or issue can actually be a blessing in disguise from the brand loyalty and credibility perspective.

You can use the opportunity for winning life-long customers by going that extra mile to upgrade shipping, offer coupons, replace their product without hassle, throw in some freebies, and other similar acts of generosity. Irate-turned-happy customers are your best brand evangelists.

Have a personality when you respond to customers. No one likes clinical, robotic, or template-like responses, especially when they are dissatisfied. Social media is for real people with unique personalities, which should come across in your responses.

It is all about connecting with people in a personal voice. HSC Advisors regularly post videos of their customer service reps to give their clients a personalized glimpse of the "real people" who handle their queries each day.

Ignore those with bad attitude. For all its virtues, one of the biggest banes of social media are the unproductive folks who barrage your posts with ugly comments.

From complaining about how pricey or ugly your products are to your business policies, they will criticize just about everything to damage your reputation. These guys have no real or specific issue. They are just there to pull you down.

You won't be able to logically explain your budgeting or policies to them since they've already made up their minds. The best thing is to simply ignore them. Don't bother getting into a drawn-out debate with them, since it will further encourage them to keep leaving nasty comments.

Creating a frequently asked questions section is a good idea. If you run a Facebook business page, you'll notice customers keep coming in with the same queries over and over. The best way to make to avoid these repetitive queries and boost customer experience is to create a handy frequently asked questions section.

Canned responses are a great way to help customers without wasting your time. Put up useful pre-written posts with relevant links, images, charts, price lists, and whatever else you think your customers might want to know.

Whenever a new customer needs help with something you've already covered, you can simply copy and paste the reply. This will save you loads of time, and help you offer swift and professional customer service to boost your credibility.

Acknowledge happy customers, too. Top notch Facebook customer experience is not just about responding to customers who have issues, but also those who are pleased with your service and take the time to say so. Don't leave the delighted folks hanging. Thank them for their positive response and the business they give you. This is a great way to keep their interaction and connection with you alive.

Take Zappos's customer service as a shining example. They respond to every post on their page, even if it's a simple "Thank You."

Exclusive Promotions for Facebook Fans

Make your Facebook fans feel special by giving them exclusive offers. Rewarding your followers is a great way to show appreciation and retain their loyalty. Create a thriving community of buyers by building a special promotional tab that only your Facebooks fans can access.

Another super way to build Facebook credibility is through praising your fans publicly by picking a 'super fan of the week' or something similar. You can send them a prize, feature them on your cover photo, or write a post sharing something unique about them and pin it to the top of your page feed. This will delight the chosen fans and impress the others.

Partner with Established Brands

This is another simple yet quick and practical tip to build brand credibility. As a small and new business, you may not have the required resources to create a brand identity from scratch.

Forging partnerships with reputed brands will give you great leverage without fancy marketing and advertising budgets. Join up with brands that share similar values by hosting a collaborative virtual event or endorse each other's content.

Partnering with established brands will lend an aura of authenticity and credibility to your brand. The exposure will also help in boosting your engagement, brand loyalty, and revenue.

Connect with the right people in the company. Start by sending them a professional mail that sets the foundation of the relationship, and explain how you can assist in achieving their brand goals. You can also use Twitter and LinkedIn to find influential brands in your domain and approach them for a mutually rewarding association. Be genuine. Tell them exactly what you can bring to the table to help them. Focus on what you can do for them rather the other way.

Patience and persistence is the key word. When you are just starting out, people may not immediately respond to your requests. However, once you have a sizeable following and decent engagement, big brands may give you an opportunity to promote your business.

Chapter 3

Using Twitter to Supercharge Brand Credibility

Basic Tweeting Guidelines

Keeps your tweets factual and professional, without bordering on dull and uninspiring. Correct spelling and grammar (even with the 140-character limit) will be the litmus test of your professionalism and attention to detail. Keep your tweets relevant to the business and company values. Add a clear profile image, which is generally your corporate or brand logo.

It is acceptable to post a few informal tweets to break the monotony and put forward a more approachable image for your followers. As a rule of thumb, your "follower" numbers should be higher than your "following" numbers i.e. the number of people following you should be greater than the number of people you follow on Twitter.

Building Credibility with Images

Include a clear, professional, and instantly identifiable image of your brand. Followers will come to recognize and associate the image with your company after a few tweets. Pictures also add a more unique personality to your account and make it stand out.

Use the Verisign logo on your profile picture. This boosts your credibility by showing buyers that you're a trusted merchant for information as well as regular products/services.

Another expert tip is to register with the Better Business Bureau or BBB. Again, this reveals that you have gone through proper legal channels for setting up your business. These images will reinforce that you are a member of registered business bodies and that you'll conduct transactions only through legitimate processes.

Use high-quality and attractive images that showcase your products and services in a flattering way. Using bright and warm shades is always a good idea for social media profile images. However, if your brand logo has predominantly cool tones, go ahead and use them as your primary tones.

Curate Customer Testimonials Using Hashtags

Customers can be encouraged to tweet experiences about your products or services using hashtags. Hashtags make your endorsement campaigns more visible and trackable. They help build a loyal customer base by boosting engagement. Existing customers share their experiences with potential customers to create a close-knit buyer community.

Keep your hashtags catchy, relevant, and unusual. Bannersnack uses #DearBannersnack brilliantly to elicit testimonials from happy customers. Use Twchat for building a public archive of customer feedback. It can be moderated as well, in the event that your hashtag becomes widespread enough to lure spammers.

Connect with Industry Leaders

Search for industry leaders in your domain to lend your campaign that extra edge. Social media big daddies have a large following, which you can benefit from. They also lend an element of credibility to your profile. Potential customers will be impressed when your brand is authenticated by the presence of a known figure within the industry.

One of the best ways to approach an influencer is to ask them an intelligent and meaningful query which hasn't already been presented to them. Do not shower them with too many kudos or you may come across as opportunistic and flattering. A few words about how and why you admire their work should suffice.

Twtrland is a great tool for finding influencers across more than 40,000 categories. You can distil searches to find the right people across topics, skills, and even countries. There are a few more focused filters on the left-hand corner. For example, you may be interested in connecting with social media experts living in a specific city.

Other handy Twtrland features include creating your list of influencers when you've found all the big names you need, and then exporting this list to an excel file. You can view the complete profile of each authority by scanning through their stats, engagement figures, and information about their most popular posts.

Buzzsumo is another free tool for locating industry leaders. It provides insights about social media's most popular content. You can search by topics (for example, travel, cooking, weight loss) or a particular blog or website to find the most shared content within the topic.

Klout is a paid service that allows users to track influencers. It can be used to research, organize, and segment influencer lists. The application assigns a Klout score to users so you can correctly pin down authorities and influencers with high Klout scores.

Combine Twitter with a Blog

Use Twitter in combination with a blog to build massive credibility. It's easy to start a regular WordPress blog. Create blog posts frequently and tweet them. A great way to get users to share your blog post is to simply add a WordPress plugin "tweet this" through the admin panel. This makes it easier for readers to tweet the posts they love. Create useful posts that people would love to share. People like to share content that makes them come across as smart and interesting within their social media circle. It validates their social standing and improves their authority signal among family and friends. Rather than constantly tweeting about your blogs or products and services, encourage other users to do it by making them look nice among their followers. This can be achieved only by creating quality and well-organized content.

Promote Talented Peers

Give an encouraging shout out to all peers who are doing wonderful work. Social media is not as much about competition as it is about fruitful collaboration.

Follow Friday (#FollowFriday) is a super Twitter custom for recommending interesting and valuable Twitter accounts. Make sure that you state the reason for the endorsement, which will help your followers know what to expect from the account's stream.

The profiles will most likely return your favor and recommend you to their followers, thus giving you more exposure and greater authority and credibility. This can also open up guest blogging opportunities, where you can get posts for your blog from other industry experts and have them feature and share you on their blogs and social networks.

Keep Growing Your Following

A large Twitter following is no vanity metric. It is a fairly reliable reflection of a person or brand's credibility or popularity. A large following indicates that a lot of people trust the brand or person enough to follow their updates.

It reveals your brand's authority, as well as the hold and influence you have on customers. For a potential customer or Twitter newbie, your number of followers gives the impression that a lot of users know you, seek you out, and follow you. It's all about impressions, and a massive following helps you create those killer impressions on prospective clients.

Keep building your following by reciprocating with follows and signing up for an effective auto-follow application like twollow or twifollow. Never ever buy Twitter followers. It can damage your credibility and reputation.

You can promote your account to interested folks using the Twitter advertising option, but avoid using services that claim to help you build a large following by buying followers. Always build and nurture a solid base of interested followers organically rather than trying to beat the system.

Tell Visually Compelling Stories

Twitter's inline pictures can boost your click-through traffic by a staggering 94%. Its 140 character tweets may seem too restrictive, but images can percolate deeper.

Utilize the power of images in sharing stories about your brand to establish a simple yet personalized connection with your audience. Create simple and interesting vignettes to share your brand values.

Be Transparent

Think about this. Has any brand or person been criticized for being polite, truthful, and transparent with their customers? Social media is all about being direct and transparent with your customers. Is there a crisis within your organization? Has business been affected? Some issues with your products or services?

Try and stay as open and genuine with your customers as possible without getting defensive or making excuses (which will only further damage your reputation). Acknowledge the problem and assure the customers that you are doing your best to iron it out. You'll come across as far more credible than if you try to push the crisis under the carpet.

Keeping your customers in the dark and coming up with fake accounts makes you look foolish when someone actually notices.

For instance, Jim Henson stated that his company had removed the promotional Kids' Meal toys from Chick-Fil-A on account of homophobic statements made by the company's top bosses. Chick-Fil-A, on the other hand, stated that the toys were actually discontinued due to safety concerns.

Amidst the debate happening on the fast food chain's wall, a woman was vociferously taking up for Chick-Fil-A. Later, another user discovered that the profile was in fact fake and the profile image being used was scooped off a stock photo site.

Chick-Fil-A obviously denied having anything to do with the profile. We don't know who was lying and who wasn't, but followers hate being hoodwinked. Nothing can damage your credibility more than misleading your followers.

Be Original

While re-tweeting relevant and useful updates can help you win a few brownie points followers, original and unique tweets are a great way to earn credibility. Be a thought leader who is known to share exciting and thought-provoking tweets. Be the go-to person for anyone who wants more information about your industry.

Keep up-to-date with trending topics, see what other influencers have to say to give it your own unique twist, back up your tweets with factual sources, share interesting industry statistics, analyze data, make seemingly complex issues easy to understand.

In short, don't be afraid to blow away followers with your knowledge. Few things scream credibility more than possessing extensive industry know-how.

Use Images Responsibly

Just because images are in the open internet domain doesn't mean copyright laws are not applicable to them. Ensure every image that is used on your account is your own or that you have legal rights from the owner of the photograph to use it. Encourage responsible image sharing to avoid damaging your credibility in copyright lawsuits. This is more real than you believe.

Take the example of band Red Jumpsuit Apparatus. They simply cropped and changed an image from their live show and put it up on social media without permission or photographer credit. What followed was an ugly and lengthy copyright spat between them and the photographer. Predictably, it earned them plenty of criticism. Eventually, they had to remove the picture, pay a sizeable sum to the photographer, and come up with an apology. They didn't receive any support and ended up with a damaged reputation and empty pockets.

Offer Sincere Customer Service

New followers and customers often see mentions about you that have been made by other users. If they see a lot of unanswered queries, issues, or negative feedback, it can give them the impression that you don't care about existing customers or followers.

Acknowledge customer complaints promptly, demonstrate empathy, and work on resolving each customer's issue. This shows you can be held accountable to your customers and makes you come across as more trustworthy and transparent.

If you find your Twitter feed being stormed with service- or complaint-related issues, it may make more sense to have a dedicated Twitter account for customer service.

Prepare Well for a Backlash

One of the perils of social media fame and popularity are haters and trolls. Because people can easily hide behind fake accounts and the impersonal nature of the internet, you may have to deal with your share of haters. The best way to deal with them is by staying true to your values and remaining unaffected. You will earn plenty of respect from your followers if you avoid retaliating each time someone slams you.

Stay true to the commitments you make to your customers, be quick in addressing their concerns, and acknowledge both positive comments and constructive criticism. This should help you stay in the good books of your followers and customers.

Encourage Warm Fuzzies

Happy customers are your best brand ambassadors. Always have the warm fuzzies rolling by acknowledging the praises and appreciation coming your way. Give back love in the form of sending your fans coupons or exclusive offers or a simple thank-you note in their mailbox.

This boosts the feel-good factor to make your brand come across as more likeable, which works wonders when it comes to recommendations. About 92% of people trust recommendations coming from people that they know. Spreading happy vibes is one of the best ways to exponentially grow your customer base.

Did you know that 50% of buyers decide to purchase something after a social media recommendation? Imagine the amount you are leaving on the table by not being nice to customers. Spread love, warm fuzzies, and happiness to make your brand more credible.

Chapter 4

Building Credibility the Big G Way

We all know the power of the big G. Google+ links to several other Google driven services that people use on an everyday basis, thus making it a vital component for boosting your brand authority. The number of users who actively consume any Google service surpasses 500 million. The sheer integration with other Google channels makes it a force to reckon with. A complete and updated profile enhances your search engine rankings and helps you reach prospective customers.

One of the best things about Google+ is that we can sort people into various circles based on multiple contexts. We have absolute control over who gets to see what we share on our Google+ timelines. It is a simple yet effective business-friendly platform. Here are some handy tips for building your credibility the Google+ way.

Build a Complete and Impressive Profile

The About Us section is a brilliant opportunity to showcase what you or your company stands for. Write in brief what your business is all about. Mention a few details about your products or services. Keep in mind that the introduction will be utilized by Google as the meta description (the page description that appears in search results).

One expert tip is to include links to various pages on your site with cleverly worded text. For example, "Social Media Expert" can be linked to a page where you've written a comprehensive and well-researched post about how beginners can leverage social media to gain more authority and influence. Ensure you use keywords judiciously and avoid keyword stuffing.

Link to other social media profiles such as your official Facebook, Twitter, and Instagram pages. A great way to gain link juice, credibility, and authority from the big G is to have your social media pages included on the G+ network. Google+ is probably the best channel for link posting. If you are a business catering to customers in a specific location, you can also include where you operate from in your business profile. This can give your credibility and exposure a big boost when people search for businesses in a particular area. Integrate your Google+ profile with other Google applications such as Google Maps or Google+ Local.

One of the biggest mistakes people and companies make on Google+ is not filling out their complete profile. Every section lets you enter information that is important from the brand and authority building perspective. Leaving any field empty would be a massive missed opportunity.

Google+ Connections

Using Google's search option, you can add lots of people to your Google+ network based on interests. Generally, people follow back the users who add them to their circle. This gives you more exposure and an opportunity to share laser targeted content with a large and interested reader base. Another credibility-boosting tip is to show off your Facebook and/or Twitter following on your Google+ profile to impress followers.

When you set up your Google + profile, ensure that the "show people who have viewed our profile" and "who have added us in their circles" options are enabled. This creates more authenticity and transparency for your brand. Create specialized circles for different content and keep sharing relevant content on each circle periodically to keep followers happy.

For instance, if you run a travel agency and have multiple customers inquiring about various tours all over the world or specific tours such as adventure holidays or eco-tourism, divide your groups based on the holidays they are interested in and post content about the sub-niches or various destinations in appropriate groups.

You can also use Google+ Hangouts (Google's very own chat service) to create a buzz about business and gain mileage by sharing vital announcements, product launches, informative webinars, interactive sessions, and several related activities for boosting your brand reputation and credibility.

Following a short introduction about you and your services, focus on creating engagement and offering value. Folks on Google+ communities love pro tips. Post helpful and industry-relevant tips for winning over followers. Ask more open-ended questions that trigger discussion, debates and analysis.

As a rule of thumb, do not spam G+ communities. Make sure you read the rules carefully before posting or you'll be kicked out by moderators, and that would be a huge blow to your credibility.

Encourage Customer Reviews

Soliciting customer reviews can be a double-edged sword. You may win some rave reviews, but a handful of folks may still use it as a platform for airing their discontent.

On the whole though, there are more pluses than minuses. Reviews lend an aura of authenticity and credibility for your brand. It shows people that you are a real business with real customers. Reviews are also great from the SEO perspective. Ensure that you don't overlook the negative reviews.

Take time to acknowledge the not so flattering reviews by responding professionally and trying to understand the customer's concern. When you actively seek reviews from customers, you'll realize that the positive reviews outnumber the negative ones by far, unless you are doing something wrong with your products or services.

If you integrate your Google+ profile with Google Maps or Google+ Local page, Google removes competitor advertisements and instead displays your enterprise when customers are actively looking for your products or services. The updated images or reviews are also immediately showcased on Google Maps. Having an up-to-date profile with a large bank of reviews can help you do well.

Connect with Established Authorities within Circles

Google+ circles are a great way to connect with authorities in your domain. For example, let's say you really admire an expert who works at an organization that you've always wanted to tie up with. If they have a public Google+ profile, you can add them to your circle. Irrespective of whether you are added by them in their network, you can still tag them with a + followed by their name.

Tag them when you have something great to share to grab their attention and entice them into a meaningful conversation. This also gives you exposure among the expert's followers, thus boosting your credibility.

Chapter 5

Instagram to the Rescue

Pictures indeed speak louder than words—especially when your promotional campaign is on a tight budget. Instagram has over 500 million active users, making it one of the largest photo sharing sites across the world. Building credibility becomes effortless if you back up whatever you are trying to communicate with images, and that's where Instagram comes to your rescue.

It leverages the power of images to create a sound identity for your business. The platform, through means of images, fosters customer loyalty and brand recognition. With its exciting interface and features, Instagram makes your products and services look more desirable. They add an interesting personality to your brand and grab the attention of users. Here are top tips to work Instagram like a boss.

Post Behind-the-Scene Glimpses

Customers love being pampered with exclusive glimpses of something no one else has access to. Posting images of your office space, employees celebrating festivals or birthdays, new products, customers, and more makes your followers feel special.

It increases a sense of belonging by making customers feel like they are a part of the organization. This increases brand loyalty. And we all know loyal customers give you way more business than new folks. Your business should be a part of the internet's photo sharing revolution or you're losing out big time!

Demonstrate the Process

Have you ever wondered what goes into the making of your favorite crop top or candy? Well, of course, and so do your customers. Just consider the popularity of the Discovery Channel's How It's Made. They unveil the most fascinating creation process for the most banal products such as toilets. This simply means that even if you don't think so, you have an extremely interesting process in place to create your products and services, which your customers may love to be introduced to.

Even if you don't manufacture anything, simply post images of new retail products or services, interesting shipments, attractive storefront displays, and others. Basically, anything that shows customers how you conduct business. You'll be surprised at the number of customers who are interested in knowing about the process behind your products and services.

Display Instagram Badges

Instagram's badges are cutesy icons given by Instagram which lets users link to other social media platforms such as Facebook, Twitter, and Pinterest. This gives customers options to interact with you through multiple networks. People will keep coming to your website, read your content, and be a part of your brand history by getting involved on multiple channels.

Post with a Plan

While randomly sharing images may reveal an interesting personality on a personal account, it may not work for a business account. Plan your image sharing campaigns and share only those images that are congruent with the overall brand vision. The aim should be to post images that boost engagement, stir discussions, trigger sharing, and drive traffic to your site.

Do not spam your feed with every image you can lay your hands on. Before posting every photo, think about how it can help you achieve your business goals.

Hashtags and Instagram Mentions

Did you know that Instagram posts with a minimum of one hashtag receive 12.6 % greater engagement than those without a hashtag? Instagram borrows the hashtag phenomenon from Twitter. They can trigger interesting and topical engagement and generate massive exposure for your brand.

You can either jump into an already thriving conversation or launch your own. Mentions are another way to draw the attention of influencers. When you mention a user (tag) with their username, it shows up on the user's feed, thus exposing the message to their followers, too.

Ensure that you use proper hashtagging etiquette. You don't want to come across as a spammer by using #kimkardashian when you aren't posting her image or have nothing to do with her. Spammers are a huge turn-off on any social media network.

Some popular hashtags on Instagram are #tbt or Throwback Thursday, the hashtag people use to post old pictures. This hashtag alone has been used in over 272 million Instagram posts. Another popular hashtag is #photofoftheday, which should be used for your best images. Hashtags give your audience an easier way to find branded content via topics and forums that are of interest to them.

Make it easy for fellow Instagrammers to locate your images by tagging the images appropriately and unambiguously. Make your photographs connect with your audience and stick out by using creative yet memorable tags. They will help you draw new followers who show a keen interest in your image, and keep your feed flourishing with likes and shares.

Come up with original and unique hashtags but ensure they are relevant to your brand. They should resonate with the tone of your brand in an interesting and compelling manner.

Hashtag competitions are great for creating a buzz. Ask your followers to post an image of themselves using your products. A few prizes can go a long way in drawing higher engagement and creating brand loyalty. Happy Instagram followers can have you laughing your way to the bank in no time.

Maintain Creativity and Professionalism

Your customers should enjoy nothing short of a stunning visual experience. There are a million images out there on the internet. What makes yours different? Convey your ideas in a creative and compelling manner by using Instagram's edit feature or using a photo editor of your choice. Instagram has a variety of filters that can present your products and services in a flattering light.

For instance, think outside the box and photograph your product in a natural backdrop rather than in a studio, or get a cute dog to hold your product in its paws rather than using a human model. People love such offbeat and cutesy images with character on Instagram.

For editing image effects, simply go to the image (either taken or uploaded from the gallery) and tap Next > Edit (bottom of your screen). You can add desired effects including Vignette, Fade, Sharpen, Brightness, Contrast, and more. For adding filters, simply tap Next, followed by the filter you want to apply. Tap Done once you're through with applying the filter. Tap Next for adding a caption to the image and sharing it. Keep your images considerably large and high in resolution.

Use the Power of Video Content

Instagram has offered individuals and businesses the power to take their visual content several notches above with the minute-long video feature. Use this brilliantly to showcase behind-the-scenes customer reactions, video testimonials, a day in your workplace, introductions to employees, after-hours fun moments for the team, and much more. Keep the approach personal, interesting, and natural. Let your audience see the faces behind the brand.

If you run an online venture or blog, create videos related to your blog content or ecommerce store. How is the merchandise packaged and readied for shipment? Or, if you run a make-up or beauty blog, you could create quick tutorial content on "Your Best Party Look in Under a Minute."

These entertaining promotions add more zing to your profile. People will lap up valuable how-to's and identify with your brand's behind-the-scenes persona. Keep the videos short and attention-grabbing, and make each second count when communicating your message.

Chapter 6

How to Build Credibility with YouTube

Did you know that YouTube is the web's second largest search engine? This means your target audience is actively seeking information and solutions for their problems on the video sharing network. Imagine the amount of money you are putting in your competitors' pockets if you do not have a YouTube presence.

A Cisco research reveals that 58% of all business web traffic will be accounted for by videos in 2017. Product video demos boost sales by about 20% to 40%. The trust factor for videos is huge and unmatched. Video content has 53 times more chances of showing up in organic search results than other media content. 35 hours of video content is uploaded onto YouTube every single minute. The phenomenon of watching videos is all the more marked now in the era of smart phones and tablets.

Here's another illuminating statistic. YouTube has over 80 million unique visitors who consume more than 4 billion video content hours each month. Several of these viewers also comment and share videos. When someone likes or shares your video on YouTube, they are in fact endorsing your content within their social network. This is far more credible than you shouting out from the rooftop about your products or services.

Here are some powerful strategies that you can weave into your credibility-building social media plan.

Use YouTube Videos to Rank Organically
YouTube video content helps you rank marvelously well if you can include the right keywords in your title and description. They give you a definite competitive edge over other content formats. Video content search results enjoy a 41% greater click-through rate. People prefer being shown how it is done than being told about it.

This should encourage you to create comprehensive, interesting, and highly optimized videos.

Here are some ways to make your videos easily findable:

1. Add your target keywords within the first few title words. An expert tip is to include a ":" after your main keyword and rephrase the title for optimal effect. For instance, your video on mortgage saving tips can be titled "Mortgage Saving Plans: 20 Tips for Financing Your New Home."

2. Make your descriptions keyword rich, interesting, and elaborate. This will make it easier for people to search for your content on YouTube. A pro tip is to begin all your descriptions with a complete URL. Include other URLs throughout the description for better targeting.

3. Ensure that all of your main and related keywords are included in the tags section. This is one of the easiest ways to be found.

Brand Your Channel

This doesn't mean you rob a bank to become a YouTube partner or sign up for a brand channel. You can create a highly brand-able platform on YouTube without spending big bucks. Here's how:

1. Create a customized background using color shades that match the overall feel of your brand. Your profile should look more lively and personalized. Nothing shakes up credibility like a default profile. A generic design makes you

appear like a shady, fly-by-night operator rather than a genuine brand that has made effort.

2. Select Player View as your video streaming layout. The Player View, as opposed to Grid View, features a single big video that is set on auto-play. Since total views can heavily influence your brand's visibility, ensure that the featured video is on Autoplay mode.

3. Create playlists for your best videos. Organize your most popular content using YouTube's playlist option. Think of using this as the YouTube counterpart of a website. Playlist along with Featured Video can be used brilliantly to make it easier for users to access your videos.

Leverage the Power of Other Social Media Networks
YouTube is not an isolated island. It can be used brilliantly in conjunction with other social media networks for greater exposure.

Create a blog for every video that is posted on YouTube. Use a keyword-focused title and include well-researched, complementing content in it. This will further boost your chances of being found through organic searches. Add easy content sharing buttons on your blog to make it simple for users to share your brilliance.

Posting the video on Facebook or Twitter is another great way to garner a greater following and higher engagement.

Submit your video to StumbleUpon, the social bookmarking website.

Post Bulletin Alerts

There's a Post Bulletin tab at the top of your YouTube channel. Use it to create a bulletin, which can be linked to videos that will appear in your subscribers' home pages. This is indeed a great way to drive traffic, attention, and engagement to your videos.

Use Trailer Videos to Convert Visitors into Subscribers

YouTube's Trailer Video feature lets you include a video right at the top of your brand's channel for nonsubscriber visitors. Use this space judiciously to let visitors know about your vision and products and services. Think of this as a magazine's cover page at a newsstand. It gives you an interesting peek into what to expect from the magazine.

Create Unconventional Videos

As the web's largest video sharing network, YouTube is quickly becoming saturated with mediocre content. Use this general mediocrity as an opportunity to stand out. Do not list out the features or benefits of your products and services in an instructional, manual-like robotic tone. People aren't watching videos on YouTube to hear mechanical infomercials.

Inject wit and humor into your videos, use creative graphics, or employ interesting analogies to explain tricky concepts. Basically, stay unconventional and do the unexpected.

Some of the most successful YouTube marketers and brand builders share original, unusual, and interesting stories. The video may or may not be directly related to your products and services, but it should convey the vibe of your brand to resonate with your target audience.

For instance, Samsung shared the video of a little girl dancing enthusiastically to promote its Galaxy 580 smart phone. They correctly recognized that people don't want monotonous videos demonstrating smart phones and their features. Rather, the company used something that had a feel of excitement and positivity to it for conveying how upbeat they were about the new launch. This helped set a happy tone for the launch, resulting in a huge number of followers clicking on the URL at the end of the video to learn more about the product.

You have to loosen folks up a bit before you inspire them to buy. Engaging people with clever videos on YouTube is great way to soften them and lead them to the desired call to action.

Create Fan Videos

Make your fans the center of attention by creating super special fan videos. Ask customers to post short videos about their experiences with your brand. Make it sound natural and genuine by including the good and not-so-good. These videos tell more personalized stories. Referrals are a great way to present your products or services to prospective customers.

You can also have contests or giveaways such as having a fan of the week or month. Subscribers can be encouraged to share video testimonials or tutorials about using your product creatively. Pick the one that gathers the most views as the winning video. There are several creative and inspiring ideas to use video content for building higher engagement and credibility.

Be Prolific and Consistent
YouTube videos are simple to make and publish, and there's no reason why you shouldn't publish at least one video per week to boost your visibility and grow your following. Naturally, the more the content you put up, the higher your visitor tally will be. Create videos that cover different angles of your products or services so you can have a channel of authority.

Chapter 7

Build Massive Credibility with LinkedIn

The common perception is that LinkedIn is only for jobseekers. This may be partly true. However, that shouldn't stop you from using the web's largest professional connection to build credibility for your brand. A professional reputation, peer recommendations, and endorsements from experts can be great for social proof. Here's how to succeed with LinkedIn.

Build an Impressive Professional Profile

This may seem obvious, but only a handful of folks get it right. Stick to a clear strategy when you're creating a LinkedIn profile. What will be your brand positioning? What skills should you highlight to your connections? In short, make your profile consistent and credible. Ensure that you fill all the fields accurately and unambiguously. Know what skills to highlight, and do not fib.

Ensure that you proofread the completed profile. Even a single typo can make your credibility plummet.

Something as basic as adding a profile photo on LinkedIn increases the chances of your profile being found by seven times. You profile picture is like an e-handshake. Keep it professional, yet friendly and approachable looking.

An optimized profile is an indication of your participation and authority within LinkedIn's ecosystem. Did you know you can make your profile twelve times more findable by including the two most recent employment positions you held?

Create a unique and attention-grabbing profile headline. The default headline is your current job or business position. It can be customized to establish your expertise in specific domains. Think of yourself as the brand and your headline as "brand you's" tagline. Headlines should capture your essence with words and a phrase used by colleagues to describe you. How about, "trusted content marketing expert" or "experienced SEO writer who's never skipped a deadline." Be specific and interesting.

Use keywords and phrases strategically to rank your profile. Select a few important keywords and sprinkle them generously in your headline and profile description. Your rank for those terms will invariably increase when users conduct a people search on the network.

LinkedIn gives you the opportunity to include up to three web URLs in your profile. Your best bet is to add your official company or brand URL or blog along with a couple of social media profiles (Twitter is good to begin with). Rather than simply labeling each link as "My Twitter Profile" or "My Blog," optimize them for search engines by giving them more keyword-focused or specific titles such as "Content Marketer's Blog" or "Social Media Expert on Twitter."

You can also alter it to the actual link titles such as the title of your blog, so that the URL is closely combined with the blog for better search engine results. This will give you a more optimized profile and make it easier for you to rank on Google.

Use Background Space Optimally

Use background space optimally for streaming content in the form of promotions, brief portfolios, images that increase your credibility, pictures, publications, and whatever else you can think of to demonstrate your expertise. Your personal brand can be decorated by utilizing images that illustrate interesting and exciting secondary interests.

For instance, you may be a travel agency operator, whose secondary skills or interests involve proficiency in foreign languages and adventure sports. This may not be your primary skill, but it adds more punch to your profile nevertheless.

One of the best pro tips to get your personal brand to rank quickly is to have a customized URL such as linkedin.com/in/fullname. It may seem more like a vanity URL; however, keep in mind that as a major professional networking site, LinkedIn rank is high on Google searches.

Answer Questions on LinkedIn

Take complete advantage of LinkedIn's answering service to flaunt your expertise. Users actually give you a chance to establish your authority and leadership in a domain.

Provide well-written, thoroughly researched, and detailed answers that reveal your hold on a particular topic. If you can include relevant content pieces to back up your answers, people will be highly impressed.

Do not give generic, vague, or worse—incorrect—answers. Nothing shatters your credibility like answering questions in an ill-informed manner on LinkedIn. If you have nothing substantial to contribute, stay quiet.

Get Recommendations Galore

Getting recommendations means someone has actually taken time to express the fact that you are a champion in what you do. This is a huge credibility boost for your brand. Recommendations are the best testimonials that help you market your business and build a desirable reputation among your customers and business community.

Ask people you've worked with to draft you a recommendation. Keep it personalized and genuine. Do not fall into the trap of sending templates to your connections for soliciting recommendations.

The ideal time to seek recommendations is just after completing a project or order for a connection. Your strengths are fresh in their mind, which will sufficiently reflect in the testimonial. Recommendations can also be sought if you've done someone a favor or if you have taken the initiative and recommended them.

Rather than focusing on several generic recommendations, target the ones that nail your exact skills. Specific skills will be more noticed and will lend a seal of greater authenticity to your brand than hackneyed strengths. You can ask people recommending you if you want certain skills highlighted and if they believe you excel in them.

Sometimes people find it tough to pin down exact skills. We can come to their rescue by helping them identify our core skills. Think from the perspective of future clients and business opportunities.

To begin with, ask for recommendations from people who know you really well and a part of your core network. These are people who have actually seen your work. Think of your ideal clients and seek recommendations from like-minded brands or customers.

Look around for people who are active and well-respected on LinkedIn. These are the influencers that can lend a massive credibility boost to your profile. Use the power of LinkedIn's communities to connect with them and ask them relevant questions. Nope, plain flattery rarely works on the social media. You have to contribute to interesting, meaningful, and intelligent discussions in order to be taken seriously by the big fish.

Avoid seeking recommendations from people who recommend every connection, as their recommendations won't hold much weight.

Publish on LinkedIn

Whether you like it or not, we live in an insanely feed-focused business world. Information is shared by the second though various channels. According to research conducted by Entrepreneur, the younger generation of professionals spends approximately 18 hours per day lapping up media in different forms.

LinkedIn's publishing platform can give you brilliant edge if you use it to generate valuable, unique, original, and thought-provoking content. There are over 3 million published posts on the platform. Witness a spike in profile visits when you start publishing on LinkedIn.

Original and well-researched content is a brilliant indication of thought leadership. You come across as someone who cares to share valuable information with others.

Dazzle with Slideshare

Did you know that over 400,000 content pieces are added into Slideshare's information sharing community every month? On an average, almost 4 million information-hungry folks visit LinkedIn SlideShare. Can you really miss incorporating it into your brand credibility building plan?

Google indexes each LinkedIn Slideshare presentation. Because over 80% of the LinkedIn Slideshare's audience comes from search engines, the presentations can award your brand a definite SEO edge. Build presentations from a unique perspective about trending topics or latest news items. These are likely to shoot up in search engines when people are looking for information on trending topics.

For instance, recently there was a lot of noise about Britain exiting from the European Union and #Brexit was trending big time all over social media. Cash in on these trends and add your own unique twist to it in the form of detailed presentations. You'll be surprised at how many folks will view your profile.

Pro Tip – Use Slideshare's clipping tool to highlight your best content. Make sure to include your presentations within your LinkedIn profile for enhancing your brand credibility.

Build Authority with LinkedIn Groups

Search for relevant groups on LinkedIn and ask to join them. Some groups are private, while others are open. Begin by briefly introducing yourself and your work. Start contributing meaningfully to discussions.

Raise pertinent questions, analyze situations from varied perspectives, share accurate statistics, and take other similar actions that add value to the group. Consistently share unique and original matter to position yourself as a thought leader.

LinkedIn groups are one of the best ways to network with experts and industry influencers. You can also ask people to share your LinkedIn Pulse published content within their network. People will share anything that makes them come across as knowledgeable and intelligent among their peers. Take advantage of this social currency syndrome and put your best content out there.

You can find targeted groups under LinkedIn's Interests option. Both groups and the Pulse Publishing platform have a powerful search feature that helps users find groups or content based on their interests.

Think outside the box when it comes to sharing content. Don't go with the "one size fits all" theory. Astute networkers know different people appreciate different content. Leverage the network's "Keep In Touch" feature (under Connections) to keep people updated about the content that would be most valuable to them.
Content that works best on LinkedIn includes unique, educational, entertaining, inspiring, and solution-focused content. Users here appreciate solutions offered in an inspiring and entertaining manner.

Another important aspect to keep in mind during group participation is respect for the group's rules. Ensure you read through the group rules after joining them. They can be viewed on the top right corner of the page. Since you will naturally be targeting the most thriving groups, rule enforcement is likely to be more stringent.

Starting your own discussions is a great way to build credibility within the group. If you consistently engage group members by initiating thought-provoking discussions, you'll soon show up as a "Top Influencer" in the group's sidebar, which is a neat trick to create exposure and authority in a busy group.

Do not initiate discussions immediately after becoming a part of the group. Spend some time participating in the busiest discussions, try to get a feel of the kind of discussions that receive most attention, and plan your first question strategically.

Understand the objectives, concerns, and aspirations of the group, and weave your discussions around it. Study the discussions initiated by the group's most popular members.

Ask for help or advice, pose a discussion question, or add a slightly controversial piece that sparks constructive debate. Your objective is to inspire as much engagement and involvement as possible.

Do not (and this is a big do not) promote your products before adding value to the group. You can post a couple of your published blogs or articles after you've earned a favorable reputation on the group by participating valuably in discussions.

Ensure that the content you post is geared toward solving a concern that members have. Don't just spam groups by posting irrelevant sales-related stuff. Social media, especially LinkedIn, is not a sales platform. It is meant to be a platform to connect with potential customers or business associates as a run-up to the sale by building relationships. Do not use it for direct selling. Engagement, rather than promotion, is key.

If you can commit to it, there's nothing like building your own information-packed LinkedIn group. This will allow you to control several aspects within the group, including selecting the discussions you want to promote the most by using the "Manager's Choice" option.

Here's how you can effectively optimize your LinkedIn group:

1. Be generous with keywords included in the group description. Make sure it sums up the essence of the group accurately. Also, add keywords within the group title so its rank on Google increases, thus giving you greater organic exposure.

2. Do not forget to include your business website or blog in the group profile. Also, include your blog's RSS feed in the group so any new post is automatically shared on each group member's home page. Get into the habit of nurturing the group by sending messages to members every week and pulling traffic to your blog or website.

3. Help others build connections by introducing people who can do business or form partnerships together. Ensure that the group successfully fills the specific needs of your target audience. This ensures that each person who joins the group is a potential lead.

Though directly promoting your products and services in groups is a huge no-no, nothing should stop you from generating leads by building more personalized relationships. Do not hesitate to build connections with people who show interest in your projects and work. You can easily connect with group members by visiting their profile and clicking on Connect.

As with any other connection message, ensure that you don't use LinkedIn's canned text. Personalize your message note to include something more meaningful and relevant about them. This makes a huge difference. Scan through their profile before you approach contacts to learn as much as possible about them. Which companies have they been employed with? What is their alma mater? Which groups do they participate in? What have they listed as their interests and hobbies? What are your mutual connections? Knowing these things will help you draft a more personalized message.

Create Power-Packed Events

Marketing an event on LinkedIn is a powerful way to gain exposure. Events can be found under the More option in the main navigation bar. This is a cool way to target hundreds of professionals without spending a dime. Host your own event and use LinkedIn to promote it.

The business networking site's viral nature allows every single connection of a user who has RSVPed the event to view it on their home page. Thus, even with a handful of RSVPs, you are potentially reaching thousands of industry folks. Answer basic queries and start endorsing the event. Send invitations to people who you think will be interested in or will benefit from your event.

Chapter 8

Using Snapchat for Business

Wondering how to use a fun social media network for business? Do you think Snapchat, the image messaging and multimedia smart phone application, isn't on the same tangent as your business? Well, think again. Snapchat has 100 million daily active visitors along with 6 billion daily video views.

Snapchat brilliantly combines the goodness of private chats with the benefits of publicly shared content. From brand networks to live events to publications, Snapchat has evolved into a powerful medium of social communication.

There are myriad creative and resourceful ways through which you can incorporate Snapchat into your social media credibility building plan. Let's sink our teeth into this fun app and discover its hidden virtues.

What Type of Content Do You Want to Share?

Like most media sharing sites, content in Snapchat can be primarily broken into value-added matter and storytelling. Decide the one that works best for your business or employ a combination of both. Here are some strategies for both these types of content to build more brand credibility.

Value Added Content
Value-added content is all about sharing useful information that focuses on educating and enlightening your audience. One of the best ways to achieve this is by sharing insider tips and techniques that you've successfully used to transform your business and achieve your business goals.

For instance, if you run a social media marketing consulting venture that helps other businesses with their social media marketing plan, you can show them the little-known tricks that helped you increase engagement and gain more traffic for a client's blog. This gives them huge value, thus boosting your authority and credibility.

Another smart tip is to show your Snapchat audience how to use industry relevant tools. Think about all the tools that your personally use that save you time and make your work more efficient.

For instance, recently Buzzsumo launched a super easy and cool Google Chrome plugin. Use the opportunity to inform your folks on Snapchat. Share your "can't do without it" tool list with users and educate them about using these tools correctly.

Offer relevant and expert tips that demonstrate your expertise in a specific field. Keep it brief, straightforward, and actionable. Share actionable tips such as, "increase your visibility by adding your social media links within your email signature." This is an easy and effective tip to boost exposure.

Other value adding content pieces include industry updates and trending news. Keep your audience in the loop by doing a daily round-up of the latest and most exciting happenings in your field.

Storytelling
Stories help build credibility, honesty, and trustworthiness for your brand. If your business isn't connecting with its target audience in the form of insider stories, you are giving away a huge chunk of your business to competitors.

Use the fun and cheery visual interface of Snapchat to create stories that reflect your company's values, vision, and culture. Buffer does this wonderfully well. The social media scheduling app consistently shares stories of their daily life scenarios and teams on Snapchat to give users a behind-the-scenes look at their organization. This invariably helps you connect with the company's values.

Snapchat audiences want something lively, timely, and interesting all the time. Give them that. Showcase your business as well as your personal life. Where do people in your company chill after hours? What are their hobbies and interests? What sports teams do they support? Snapchat allows for a more personal interface. Use this to humanize your brand and make it more likeable.

Share event-based stories (events you attend or host) in different phases to inform and educate your Snapchat audience. This not just gives you an opportunity to share your brand's story but also creates greater engagement. You can break the content down into three main areas, including the pre-event buzz that triggers curiosity about the event among your audience. The 'during' event updates can include compelling keynotes, fun activities, and exhibitors, and so on. Lastly, the after events can focus on the most important takeaways from the event in the form of post-event analysis, discussions, comments, and an important call-to-action.

Build a Laser-Targeted Audience
Here are some super cool and highly effective ways to build a powerful Snapchat following.

One of the best ways to leverage Snapchat is to utilize the following you have built on other social networks. To begin it, create something meaningful that your audience can relate to and find useful. Download your Snapchat built story and share it on other social platforms. Do not forget to include a Snapchat profile link. This way the following you have built on other platforms can connect with you on Snapchat.

To do this, first go to the Snapchat story that you want to share with others and tap on Download. Swipe down the camera screen option and select Add Friends. Go to Share User Name next, followed by Copy. Lastly, upload your Snapchat video on other networks and include your Snapchat profile link.

Another way to grow your Snapchat following is by doing a comprehensive search on other social media platforms. For instance, use Twitter's Advanced Search and look for the "Add me on Snapchat" option. Fill the boxes according to what is applicable to your target users. You can target people based on interests or location. Mention precise phrases and words to make your searches more relevant.

Add Snapchat users and keep them engaged. Send them an interesting snap introducing yourself and giving them a brief sentence about your business or interests. Ask them meaningful questions, comment on others' stories, or send a personalized direct message.

Ghostcodes is a wonderful app for gaining visibility and growing your Snapchat following. It allows you to create a profile, choose relevant categories, and find fellow Snapchat users in focused categories. Users can also rank you using the heart icon.

To begin with, download the Ghostcodes app. Tap the settings button for setting up a profile. You can locate other similar users, rate them, and directly download their unique Snapcodes.

Running competitions on Snapchat is a cool and interesting way to build following. Make it clear that users have to follow you to be eligible for the competition. Share your Snapchat profile link through the competition. It will be easier for people to participate. Gleam is a cool app that allows you to create a variety of social media competitions, which can also be embedded on your blog or website through an attractive widget.

Use every available chance to spread your unique snapcode and Snapchat username. In other words, just hustle aggressively to help more people notice your Snapchat presence. Think differently! How about including your Snapcode on a business card? Unusual? Yes. Gives you exposure? Big time yes.

Engage Your Audience
As with every other social media platform, your job doesn't end by simply building an enviable following. In fact, the real job starts now when you have to retain the following by keeping them engaged and interested. Engagement is the key when it comes to converting followers into loyal customers. Here are some effective strategies to engage your Snapchat followers.

Ask questions. Questions are really the best way to get your audience 'talking.' Ensure the questions you raise are meaningful and industry-relevant. Come up with prompt responses for users who reply. You can ask about for their views or opinions about some aspect described in your Snapchat story, or conduct an opinion poll on something vital discussed in the story.

Another expert user engagement strategy is to encourage users to create interesting snaps and share them with you. Make them feel special by featuring these in your Snapchat stories. Inform your audience that they need to download their snap and share the video via email. You can then pick favorites and include them in your stories.

Analyzing Snapchat Performance

To be able to tweak your Snapchat strategies, drive engagement and create spectacular results, you have to be able to measure performance. Here are two crucial Snapchat performance measuring metrics.

1. *Total story completions* – This gives you the tally of users who have seen your entire story. It is listed right next to your most recent story video.

2. *Story completion ratio* – This is nothing but the percentage of people who viewed your Snapchat story but didn't watch in its entirety. This is a vital performance

measurement metric because a poor story completion ratio means users abandoning your content, which means it may not be interesting enough for them. This gives you the opportunity to analyze your content and know why it is not appealing to your target users enough to keep them hooked until the end. It also shows you which content is faring well.

Conclusion

Thank you for downloading *Social Media Marketing: Tips + Tricks to Increase Credibility*.

I really hope this book helped you understand the finer nuances for building credibility and trustworthiness with social media marketing. The aim is to offer you to-the-point, simple, and actionable nuggets of wisdom that can massively boost your credibility.

I hope this book inspired you to create your own innovative strategies for striking it big in the social media realm. There are several other methods than can be built around the strategies listed in the book. Just think outside the box, keep experimenting and fine tuning your techniques, and analyze what works best for your business.

The next step is to TAKE ACTION. As Mark Twain famously said, "The man who does not read has no advantage over the man who cannot read." Knowledge without application is as good as lack of knowledge.

Begin by creating a comprehensive social media plan in line with your business goals. See where your audience hangs out, engage with them, boost your visibility, and attract traffic to your website or blog. Brands are not built overnight.

It takes dedication, persistence, consistency, and effort to build credibility. But guess what? Once you jump in by taking action, everything falls in place. Just start by taking action today.

Finally, if you enjoyed this book, then I'd like to ask you for a favor, would you be kind enough to leave a review for this book on Amazon? It'd be greatly appreciated!

Thank you and good luck!

Other books by E J Scott

Content Marketing *(A Beginner's Guide to Dominating the Market with Content Marketing)*

Content Marketing *(Strategies to Capture and Engage your Audience, while Quickly Building an Authority)*

Content Marketing *(Tips and Tricks to Increase Credibility)*

Email Marketing *(Beginner's Guide to Dominating the Market with Email Marketing)*

Email Marketing *(Strategies to Capture and Engage your Audience, while Quickly Building Authority)*

Email Marketing *(Tips and Tricks to Increase Credibility)*

www.ingramcontent.com/pod-product-compliance
Lightning Source LLC
Chambersburg PA
CBHW071252220526
45468CB00001B/100